2003 MASTERS ANNUAL

Published by Augusta National Golf Club
Copyright © 2003 Augusta National Golf Club
www.masters.org

CONTENTS 2003

2003 MASTERS ANNUAL

4 MESSAGE FROM THE CHAIRMAN

6 MONDAY - WEDNESDAY
Will History Reign at the Masters?
Tiger Woods is chasing an unprecedented third Masters victory in a row.

18 FIRST ROUND
Clarke Beats Elements to Lead First Round
Spain's Sergio Garcia and amateur Ricky Barnes trail by three strokes on a day when survival was key.

33 SECOND ROUND
Weir's Mental Strength Provides Masters Edge
The Canadian believes mental toughness is the hardest part of leading.

44 THIRD ROUND
Soft Spoken Maggert Efficiently In Control
Although he's been one of the game's top technicians, Jeff Maggert is looking for his first major championship.

60 FOURTH ROUND
It's No Left-handed Compliment; Weir's Stellar Play Wins Masters
Every time Mike Weir needed to make a crucial putt in the final round he did en route to victory.

77 THE CHAMPION
Oh, Canada!
Mike Weir becomes the first Canadian and the first left-handed golfer to ever win the Masters Tournament.

81 RESULTS & STATISTICS

Published by Pachyderm Press, Inc.
P.O. Box 661016 • Birmingham, AL 35266-1016 • 205/822-4139
www.pachydermpress.com

EDITOR/PUBLISHER Wallace Sears   DESIGN Angie H. Miller
WRITER Richard Mudry
PHOTO EDITOR/ PHOTOGRAPHER Sam Greenwood
PHOTOGRAPHERS Rusty Jarrett, Pat McDonogh
ADMINISTRATION Shelly Marks

Photographic Assistance Provided by Nikon Professional Services
Printed in Canada by Friesens
ISBN 1-931656-06-1

2003 MASTERS • AUGUSTA NATIONAL GOLF CLUB

Message from the Chairman

From its inception, the Masters Tournament has truly been an international event. Some of our most poignant and dramatic moments have come from our international contestants. This year, our neighbor to the North, Canada, was well represented by an outstanding player.

Mike Weir's gutsy putting and pinpoint iron play contributed to one of the most memorable Masters finishes in recent memory. Mike's clutch par-saving putt at the 72nd hole led to the Tournament's first playoff in 13 years.

Credit must also be given to runner-up Len Mattiace. Len played spectacular golf on Sunday, including an eagle at No. 13, and scored a 65, one stroke shy of the best Masters final round ever. I would also like to recognize Tiger Woods. Although Tiger did not capture an historic third consecutive Green Jacket, he has been a great champion.

I hope you enjoy this year's Masters Annual, and on behalf of Augusta National Golf Club I would like to thank everyone for a successful 2003 Masters. I look forward to the 2004 Tournament that will be contested April 5-11.

Hootie Johnson

2003 MASTERS • AUGUSTA NATIONAL GOLF CLUB

MONDAY-WEDNESDAY

Will History Reign at the Masters?

Tiger Woods is chasing an unprecedented third Masters victory in a row.

Nothing excites the true Masters patron more than the chance to witness history in the making.

Mention the Masters Tournament and Tiger Woods in the same sentence and you've got a recipe for a tournament of epic proportions.

So when the 93-player field assembled at Augusta National Golf Club in April, all the ingredients were in place for another memorable Masters.

Woods was seeking an unprecedented third consecutive title, something none of the great Masters champions had been able to accomplish since the event started in 1934.

But Mother Nature had other ideas. She balked at providing sunny, blue skies to start the week.

The 67th edition of golf's annual rite of spring began with an uncharacteristic soggy start.

A stubborn low-pressure system from the west blanketed the Augusta National Golf Club Monday and began a three-day odyssey that hampered player preparation and washed out one entire practice round.

Monday was washed away by more than 1.3 inches of rain, according to the National Weather Service. With severe weather in the area, including lightning, Masters Tournament officials opted not to open the course to spectators.

The decision marked the first time in 20 years that an entire day was washed away by inclement weather.

And with more precipitation on the horizon, the players knew that the rain-drenched 7,290-yard, par-72 layout would still require a golfer to hit it straight, play pinpoint irons and sink crucial putts.

Masters Tournament Chairman of the Competition Committees Will F. Nicholson Jr., admitted the storied layout was nearly saturated.

"The golf course has taken as much water as it can take," Nicholson said Wednesday on the eve of the first round of the Tournament. "We have mowed the greens. Double cut all of the greens every day. We have made arrangements and have hired in the local community 31 hand-pushed mowers and we'll

Masters champions Gary Player, Jack Nicklaus and Arnold Palmer, were a featured grouping in the traditional Par 3 Contest Wednesday. The trio has won 13 Masters titles.

Tiger Woods, a three-time Masters champion, used a little body English to try and coax a putt into the hole. Woods missed the birdie putt during the Par 3 Contest.

mow the landing areas on the fairways or in the second cut, but we'll have it so it's fair in the fairways."

Augusta National, said Nicholson, had redone the bunkers four times through Wednesday.

Augusta National, lengthened 285 yards in 2002 requires precise iron play to the correct portion of the undulating greens.

Only one course change occurred in 2003. The par-4 fifth hole was lengthened 20 yards to 455 yards with the tee extended and the re-measurement of the dogleg. Bunkers on the left side of the fairway were deepened to penalize errant shots and moved 80 yards toward the green, and the fairway was narrowed to place a greater premium on driving accuracy. The changes were made to put teeth back into one of Augusta National's traditionally most difficult holes.

Add in three days of rain and soft fairways and it seemed the perfect recipe for long hitters.

"Today's practice round played as long as I've ever seen it," said left-hander Phil Mickelson.

"With colder temperatures and soft fairways you aren't able to fly the ball to the (fairway) plateaus or over the peaks of the hills. But these are conditions that give the player the chance to score the best. Although it's playing long, you have soft greens and they are greens that you can attack and get the ball stopped close to the hole, as well as be aggressive putting them."

With Woods aiming at an unprecedented three Masters Tournament titles in a row, the stage was set for a historical week.

After all, only three players, Jack Nicklaus, Nick Faldo and Woods, have won two Masters titles in a row in the history of the event.

Nicklaus, a six-time Masters Tournament winner,

Justin Leonard, right, and Hannah Verplank, daughter of Masters invitee Scott Verplank, share a moment during the Par 3 Contest.

Davis Love III was expected to be among the contenders.

PAR 3 CONTEST
CLOSEST TO THE HOLE

1.	Gary Player	82"
2.	Davis Love III	Hole-In-One
3.	Len Mattiace	6"
4.	Scott McCarron	32"
5.	Vijay Singh	41"
6.	Fred Couples	31"
7.	David Duval	8"
8.	Ben Crenshaw	14"
9.	Gary Player	4"

collected his back-to-back titles in 1965-66. He surprised everyone by missing the 36-hole cut in his 1967 attempt for a third in a row. Gay Brewer captured his Green Jacket that year.

Faldo collected his two titles in 1989-90, both in two-hole playoffs, but while his 1991 attempt at Masters Tournament history was better than Nicklaus', it was not enough to break the record-tying deadlock. Faldo finished tied for 12th, five strokes behind Welshman Ian Woosnam.

So that left Woods contemplating a possible rendezvous with history.

He knew the importance of the week and so did those who were also trying to win the prestigious title.

Woods' professional history at Augusta National is impressive.

He's won three times, including by a record 12 strokes over Tom Kite in 1997 with a 18 under par 270 aggregate, and owns or shares 18 scoring records.

Moreover, Woods entered the 2003 Masters Tournament with the record for the most consecutive sub-par rounds (10) from 2000-2002.

There was no unconditional surrender by the remaining 92 players in the field. But they knew Woods was the man to beat and the possibility boggled the mind of at least one former winner, Gary Player.

"If Tiger wins three in a row," said Player, "it will leave an indelible mark in (golf) history."

"Tiger will always be there," said Spaniard Sergio Garcia in the run-up to Thursday's first round.

"If he plays well, there's no doubt he'll be up there."

"Tiger is very much like what Jack Nicklaus was," said U.S. Open champion Retief Goosen.

"He's able to really block out everything that's going on around him. And his focus and concentration is so good that he can calm himself out there under these situations very easily."

Woods, who owns one of the strongest games and minds in the history of golf, knew the significance facing him.

"I would really like to win this week," said Woods. "It would be huge to win three Masters. No one's ever done it before. And I've been able to do certain things in golf that

(Above): Augusta native Charles Howell III tested his iron game before the Par 3 Contest on the Tournament course. (Bottom left): Gary Player's tee shot at No. 9 during the Par 3 Contest settled four inches from the hole and an Augusta National Golf Club member was happy to let everyone know. (Bottom right): Patrons at the Par 3 course enjoyed a beautiful panoramic view of the 1,060-yard, Par 3 Contest which annually is the final event before Tournament play begins.

no one's ever done before. If you're ever in that position, you want to take advantage of it because it doesn't happen all the time."

So was he the favorite, Woods was asked.

"I guess I'm still the favorite," said Woods, smiling.

With inclement weather surrounding the event early in the week, a longer-playing Augusta National Golf Club, and Woods' race to history, Masters activities began with the annual Par 3 Contest Wednesday.

The Par 3 Contest suffered a somewhat similar fate at the hands of the weather, however.

Ireland's Padraig Harrington and American David Toms were declared co-winners when afternoon storm cut short the competition.

Harrington and Toms each shot 6-under-par 21 over the 1,060-yard course.

Only Davis Love III made a hole-in-one on the day, the 51st ace in the 43-year history of the Par 3 competition.

Even the youngest of caddies at the Par 3 Contest need to take a break from the action sometimes.

MASTERS HISTORY

5 Years Ago: Mark O'Meara birdied three of the final four holes to become the oldest first-time Masters champion at the age of 41 years 2 months 30 days. He also set the standard for the most attempts (15) before a Masters first win. He became the first player since Arnold Palmer in 1960 to birdie the final two holes and claim victory.

10 Years Ago: Aided by an eagle at No.13 and a birdie at No.15, Bernhard Langer became the 12th Masters winner with mutliple titles.

15 Years Ago: Using a 7-iron out of the fairway bunker at No. 18, Sandy Lyle defeated Mark Calcavecchia by one stroke. It was the second time (Arnold Palmer, 1960) a final birdie putt won the Masters.

20 Years Ago: This was the last time the Tournament was forced to a Monday finish. Seve Ballesteros opened the final round birdie-eagle-par-birdie on the way to his second Masters title in four years. It also marked the first year the players had the option of using their own caddie.

25 Years Ago: Gary Player tied the record for the low final round (64) which included seven birdies on the final ten holes, gaining him his third Masters title. Player started the final round seven shots behind leader Hubert Green and scored a second nine 30 for a one stroke win. The patron badge waiting list was also closed that year.

30 Years Ago: Forced to a Monday finish, Tommy Aaron scored a final round 68 to erase a four stroke deficit becoming the second Georgia native to win the Tournament. Television coverage was extended to hole No.12, and it was the first delayed television broadcast to Japan.

35 Years Ago: Bob Goalby birdied Nos. 13 and 14 and eagled No. 15 for a final round score 66. Roberto De Vicenzo signed an incorrect scorecard and missed a playoff.

40 Years Ago: Jack Nicklaus defeated Tony Lema by one stroke to win his first Green Jacket. Veterans Julius Boros (43 years old) and Sam Snead (50) finished two stokes back.

45 Years Ago: Arnold Palmer won his first Masters, aided by an eagle on No. 13 during the final round. The term 'Amen Corner' was first used by Herbert Warren Wind to describe where the action had occurred on the final day. Par 3 course was built, Nelson and Hogan Bridges constructed and dedicated.

50 Years Ago: Ben Hogan scored a 72-hole total 14-under-par 274, breaking the Tournament scoring record by five strokes, to win his second Green Jacket. Hogan became the first Masters participant to score three rounds under 70. Press building Quonset hut erected and Eisenhower Cabin built.

PAR 3 CONTEST WINNERS

Year	Winner	Score
2003	Padraig Harrington	21
	David Toms	21
2002	Nick Price	22
2001	David Toms	22
2000	Chris Perry	23
1999	Joe Durant	22
1998	Sandy Lyle	24
1997	Sandy Lyle	22
1996	Jay Haas	22
1995	Hal Sutton	23
1994	Vijay Singh	22
1993	Chip Beck	21
1992	Davis Love III	22
1991	Rocco Mediate	24
1990	Ray Floyd	23
1989	Bob Gilder	22
1988	Tsuneyuki Nakajima	24
1987	Ben Crenshaw	22
1986	Gary Koch	23
1985	Hubert Green	22
1984	Tommy Aaron	22
1983	Hale Irwin	22
1982	Tom Watson	23
1981	Isao Aoki	22
1980	Johnny Miller	23
1979	Joe Inman Jr.	23
1978	Lou Graham	22
1977	Tom Weiskopf	23
1976	Jay Haas	21
1975	Isao Aoki	23
1974	Sam Snead	23
1973	Gay Brewer	20
1972	Steve Melnyk	23
1971	Dave Stockton	23
1970	Harold Henning	21
1969	Bob Lunn	23
1968	Bob Rosburg	22
1967	Arnold Palmer	23
1966	Terry Dill	22
1965	Art Wall	20
1964	Labron Harris Jr.	23
1963	George Bayer	23
1962	Bruce Crampton	22
1961	Deane Beman	22
1960	Sam Snead	23

2003 MASTERS TOURNAMENT INVITEES

Tommy Aaron (1)
Robert Allenby (Australia)(14,16,17)
Stuart Appleby (Australia)(13,14,16,17)
George Archer (1)
Severiano Ballesteros (Spain)(1)
#* Ricky Barnes (6-A)
Rich Beem (4,14,16,17)
Thomas Bjorn (Denmark)(16,17)
Gay Brewer (1)
Jack Burke (1)
Jonathan Byrd (14)
Tom Byrum (11)
Angel Cabrera (Argentina)(10,16,17)
Chad Campbell (15)
Michael Campbell (New Zealand)(16,17)
Billy Casper (1)
K. J. Choi (Korea)(14,16,17)
Tim Clark (South Africa)(17)
Darren Clarke (N. Ireland)(16,17)
Charles Coody (1)
John Cook (14)
Fred Couples (1)
Ben Crenshaw (1)
Chris DiMarco (10,14,16,17)
David Duval (3,16,17)
Steve Elkington (Australia)(13)
Ernie Els (South Africa)(3,10,14,15,16,17)
Bob Estes (14,16,17)
Nick Faldo (England)(1,10,11)
Niclas Fasth (Sweden)(16,17)
Brad Faxon (10,14,16,17)
Raymond Floyd (1)
Doug Ford (1)
Fred Funk (12,14,16,17)
Jim Furyk (14,15,16,17)

Sergio Garcia (Spain)(10,11,14,16,17)
Bob Goalby (1)
Retief Goosen (South Africa) (2,10,14,16,17)
Jay Haas (15,17)
Padraig Harrington (Ireland)(10,11,16,17)
Scott Hoch (11,14,15,16,17)
Charles Howell III (14,16,17)
John Huston (17)
Toshi Izawa (Japan)(16)
Lee Janzen (2)
Miguel Angel Jimenez (Spain)(10)
Shingo Katayama (Japan)(16)
Herman Keiser (1)
Jerry Kelly (14,16,17)
Bernhard Langer (Germany)(1,16,17)
#* Alejandro Larrazabal (Spain)(7)
Paul Lawrie (Scotland)(3,16)
Tom Lehman (17)
Justin Leonard (12,14,15,16,17)
Thomas Levet (France)(13)
Peter Lonard (Australia)(16,17)
Davis Love III (5,10,14,15,16,17)
Steve Lowery (14,16,17)
Sandy Lyle (Scotland)(1)
Jeff Maggert (11)
#* Hunter Mahan (6-B)
Shigeki Maruyama (Japan)(10,14,16,17)
Len Mattiace (14)
Billy Mayfair (11)
Scott McCarron (14,16,17)
Rocco Mediate (14,16,17)
Phil Mickelson (10,11,14,16,17)
Larry Mize (1)
Colin Montgomerie (Scotland)(10,16,17)
#* Ryan Moore (8)

Byron Nelson (1)
Jack Nicklaus (1)
Jose Maria Olazabal (Spain)(1,10,14,16)
Mark O'Meara (1,3)
Arnold Palmer (1)
Craig Parry (Australia)(14,16,17)
Pat Perez (14)
Craig Perks (New Zealand)(5,14)
Kenny Perry (14,16,17)
Gary Player (South Africa)(1)
Nick Price (Zimbabwe)(11,14,16,17)
Chris Riley (12,14,16,17)
Loren Roberts (14)
John Rollins (14)
Eduardo Romero (Argentina)(16,17)
Justin Rose (England)(16,17)
Adam Scott (Australia)(10,16,17)
Vijay Singh (Fiji)(1,4,10,14,15,16,17)
Jeff Sluman (14,16,17)
Craig Stadler (1)
Kevin Sutherland (14)
Toru Taniguchi (Japan)(16)
Phil Tataurangi (New Zealand)(14)
David Toms (4,14,16,17)
Kirk Triplett (17)
Scott Verplank (16,17)
Tom Watson (1)
Mike Weir (Canada)(15,16,17)
Tiger Woods (1,2,3,4,5,12,14,15,16,17)
Ian Woosnam (Wales)(1)
#* George Zahringer (9)
Fuzzy Zoeller (1)

Number after each name indicates the basis of qualification. See qualifications on next page. The Masters Committee, at its discretion, also invites International players not otherwise qualified.
 # Denotes First Masters
* Denotes Amateur

QUALIFICATIONS
FOR INVITATION

1. Masters Tournament Champions (Lifetime)
2. US Open Champions (Honorary, non-competing after 5 years)
3. British Open Champions (Honorary, non-competing after 5 years)
4. PGA Champions (Honorary, non-competing after 5 years)
5. Winners of The Players Championship (3 years)
6. Current US Amateur Champion (6-A) (Honorary, non-competing after 1 year) and the runner-up (6-B) to the current US Amateur Champion
7. Current British Amateur Champion (Honorary, non-competing after 1 year)
8. Current US Amateur Public Links Champion
9. Current US Mid-Amateur Champion
10. The first 16 players, including ties, in the 2002 Masters Tournament
11. The first 8 players, including ties, in the 2002 US Open Championship
12. The first 4 players, including ties, in the 2002 PGA Championship
13. The first 4 players, including ties, in the 2002 British Open Championship
14. The 40 leaders on the Final Official PGA Tour Money List for 2002
15. The 10 leaders on the current year Official PGA Tour Money List published during the week prior to the 2003 Masters Tournament
16. The 50 leaders on the Final Official World Golf Ranking for 2002
17. The 50 leaders on the Official World Golf Ranking published during the week prior to the 2003 Masters Tournament.

(Opposite page): Masters patrons enjoy taking their pictures in front of the stately white Augusta National Golf Club Clubhouse.
(Left): Korea's K.J. Choi gave his 5-year-old son David a helping hand with his clubs during a lighter moment in the Par 3 Contest.

What They're Saying

"I do like playing in tough (Masters) conditions. That doesn't mean you always play well, but I enjoy the challenge."
- *Tiger Woods, three-time Masters champion, on why he enjoys Augusta National Golf Club.*

"I miss him giving you a tip or whatever it might be or one of his jokes sometimes. But I think that the world of golf will sorely miss Sam Snead."
- *Arnold Palmer, four-time Masters champion, on the May 2002 death and absence of legendary Sam Snead from the Tournament this year.*

"If I go back and look at the last time that I really had a golf swing and a golf game that I felt like I could rely upon with my old muscle memory of what I grew up with, oh, it was probably back in the mid 90s. I was in my 50s."
- *Jack Nicklaus, six-time Masters Champion, discussing how he's trying to find his golf game after hip replacement surgery several years ago which caused him to miss the 1999 Masters.*

What They're Writing

As Dave McNeilly, caddie to Padraig Harrington, walked the Augusta National course yesterday he could hear, at every green, a humming, whirring sort of noise which, mysteriously, seemed to be coming from under the ground.

At first McNeilly put the sound down to his undeniably overactive imagination but it later transpired not only to be quite real, but the reason why he and the Irishman Harrington were able to walk the course at all. What he heard was noise from the machines that have saved the 2003 Masters.

Given that about two inches of rain has fallen in the area in the past two days, the golf club would normally be saturated, and closed.

But this is Augusta National and this is the US Masters and the men who run the major have determined that mere rain, albeit buckets of the stuff, is not going to stop either the tournament or the players' preparation for it.

So they have installed, under every green and in certain key collection points on the course, machines called SubAir. These machines act like giant, reversible, underground vacuum cleaners, able at the touch of a switch to either suck water from a given area or blow warm air into it.

- *David Davies*
The London Guardian

Ernie Els took one last look at the rain puddling at his feet just before he took cover in the locker room at Augusta National Golf Club.

"I've never seen weather like this in a major," he said.

Welcome to Water World, or whatever you want to call the rain-drenched 67th Masters, where the first round was called off Thursday for the first time since 1939. The last time any round of the Masters couldn't be played because of rain was 1983, when the second round was washed out.

"I told friends last year that I'd never seen it like this," Lee Janzen said. "I said, 'You'll never see it like this again.' I was wrong. It's worse this year. I think the guys are prepared to play Monday."

- *Thomas Bonk*
The Los Angeles Times

It seems as if he has been around forever but, admit it, you have socks stuffed in the back of the drawer that are older than Sergio Garcia.

He was a scratch golfer at age 13, won the European Amateur at 15, played in the British Open at 16 and triumphed in a pro tournament at 17. Garcia has career earnings of $7.2 million on the PGA Tour, which doesn't include all the Euros and pounds and rials and yen he has banked.

He's 23 years old.

So what's the hurry? Who cares that he hasn't won a major championship?

- *Dave Hackenburg*
Toledo Blade

(Opposite page): Playing in his tenth Masters, South African Ernie Els hoped to better his second place finish in 2000. (Above): David Toms and Padraig Harrington shot 6-under-par 21s over the nine-hole course. (Below): Two-time Masters champion Tom Watson sharpened his putting skills.

Did You Know?

- This year 40 players broke a Masters record for the most international players in the field. The previous mark of 37 was set in 2001 and 2002.

- If you're wondering who has played the most Masters without winning, it was Gene Littler and Tom Kite. Both have played 26 times.

- In the history of the Masters, Tiger Woods already holds a special place after competing in eight events, six as a professional. Woods, 27, has won eight major championships and three of them are the Masters. That ranks Woods tied for third with four other Masters champions. They include three-time champions Jimmy Demaret, Sam Snead, Gary Player and Nick Faldo. Only Jack Nicklaus (six) and Arnold Palmer (four) have won more Masters

- In the history of the Masters three players have finished second in their first Masters and never were able to improve upon that. Lloyd Mangrum, who finished second in 1940 played in 20 Masters, Tony Lema, was second in 1963 and competed in four Masters, and Dan Pohl, who finished second in 1982 and played in seven Masters were never able to finish better than their debuts.

- Since World War II eight Masters champions have shot the low opening nine-hole score and gone on to win. The last time it happened was in 1982 when Craig Stadler shot 35 and was tied with six others.

- In the 66 Masters played only three winners have become champions in their first attempt. Horton Smith won the first Masters in 1934 and Gene Sarazen won in his first attempt a year later. Fuzzy Zoeller was the last first time winner in 1979. That came via a playoff.

2003 MASTERS • AUGUSTA NATIONAL GOLF CLUB

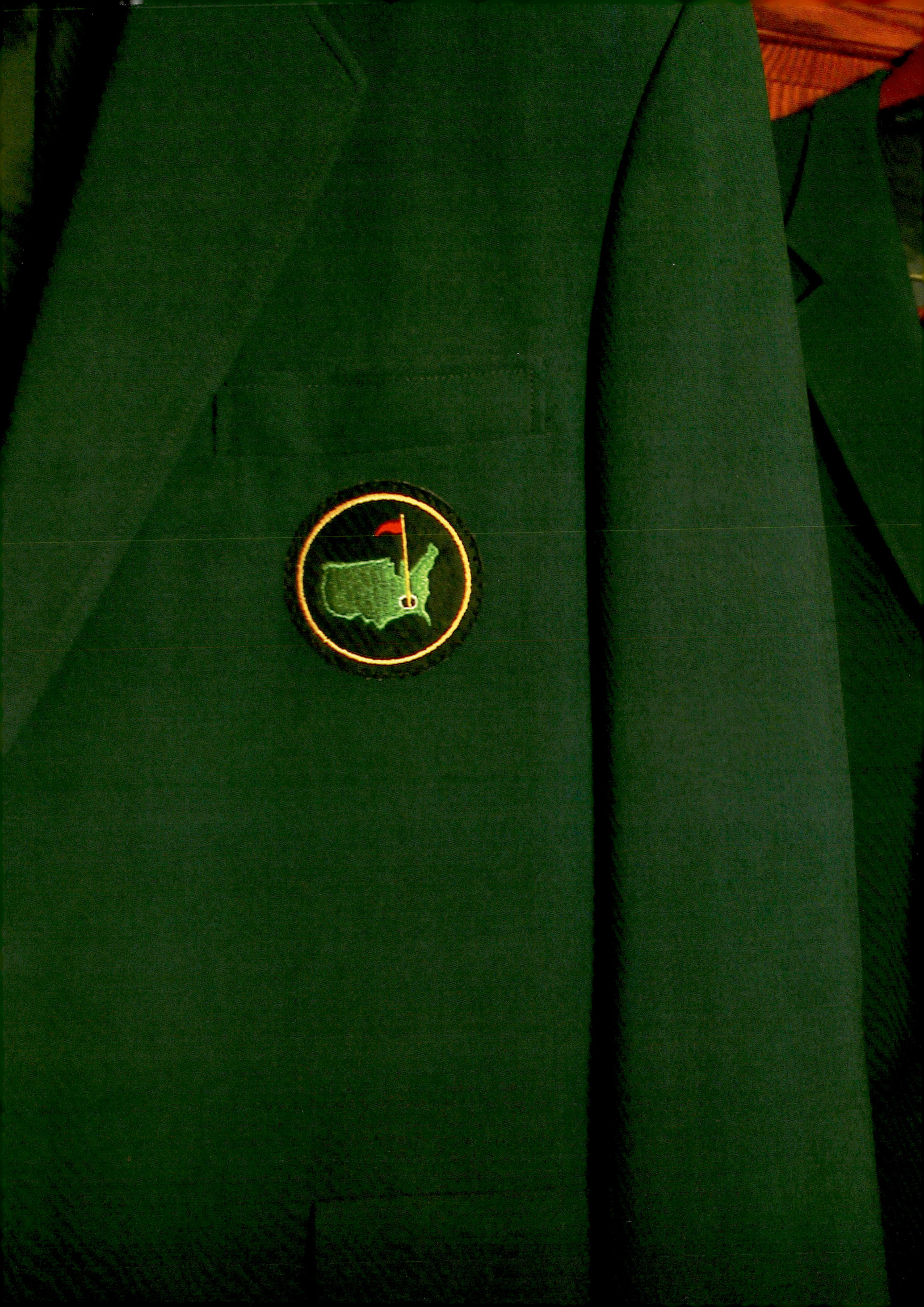

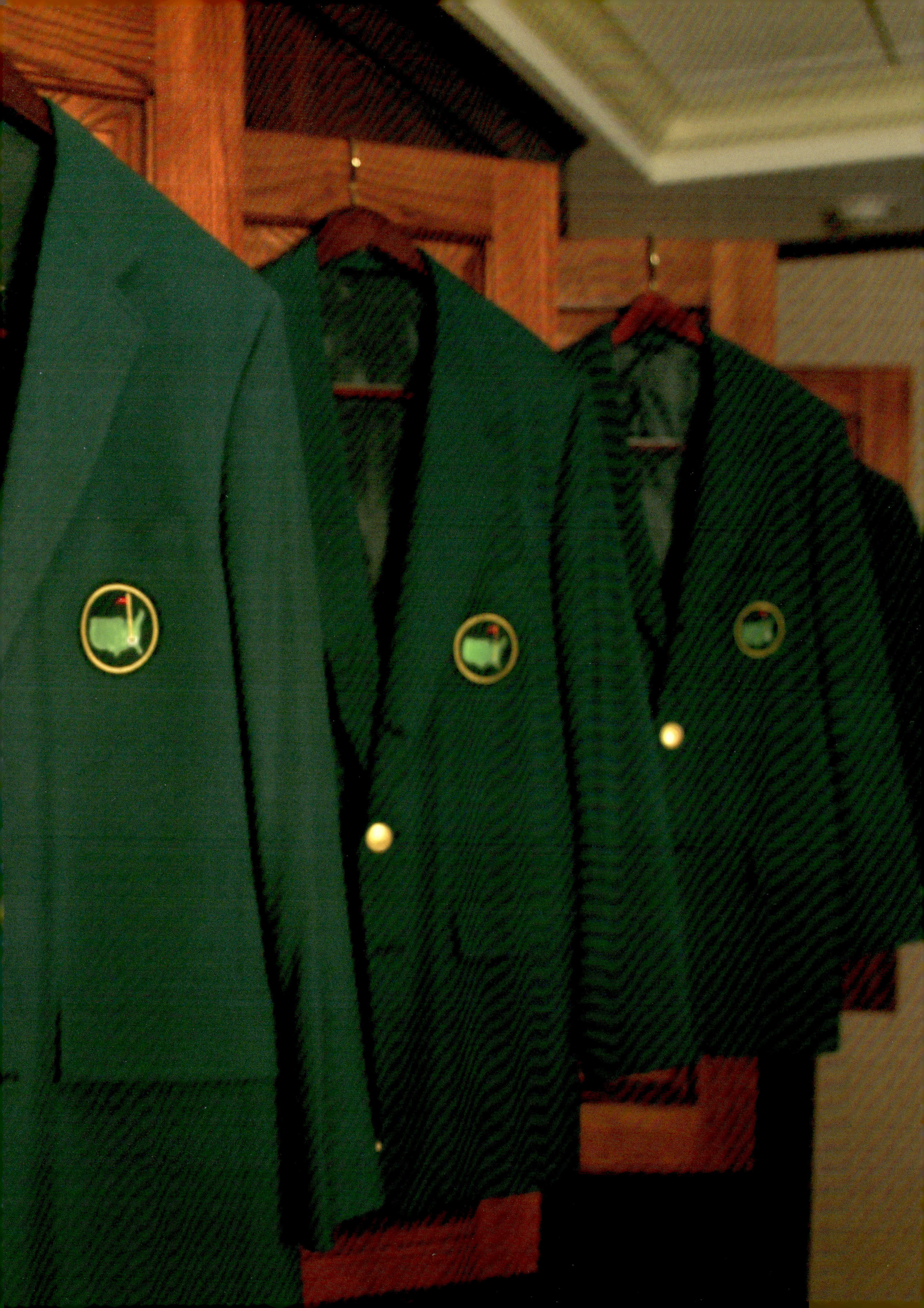

ROUND ONE 2003

Clarke Beats Elements To Lead First Round

Spain's Sergio Garcia and amateur Ricky Barnes trail by three strokes on a day when survival was key.

One by one they came walking up the hill toward the Augusta National Golf Club Clubhouse.

Their eyes were glazed over or vacant in some cases. Their faces were ruddy-colored from the morning chill of the first round.

And the patience of some of the field may have been wearing thin. After all, the first round was delayed a day by rain, forcing Masters officials to schedule 36 holes of competition on Friday. Slate-gray skies, morning temperatures in the 40s, a bothersome bone-chilling wind, and the prospects of a 36-hole day did little to put happy faces on those battling the course.

The first round, delayed a day because of the first first-round washout since 1939, had begun under difficult conditions and the players knew the next Masters champion was in for a full examination of his game.

With the rain-soaked fairways offering little roll off the tee and the scores soaring into the stratosphere, under-par numbers were worth their weight in gold.

In all, seven players finished under par.

Of those, the spot at the top of the Masters leader board belonged to Northern Ireland's Darren Clarke at six-under-par 66.

"It was obviously very good," said Clarke about his first 18 holes. "The 66 was a pretty fair score. I hit it close a lot."

Clarke, one of the premier players on the PGA European Tour, was No. 23 in the World Golf Rankings entering the Masters, and had played in six events on the PGA Tour and European Tour.

Sergio Garcia of Spain, an eighth place finisher in 2002, was tied for second with U.S. Amateur champion Ricky Barnes. Both shot three-under-par 69s.

Nick Price and Canadian Mike Weir posted 70s and David Toms and Toru Taniguchi signed cards for 71.

Four players were at even par 72 and 15 scores were 80 or higher.

None of those at par or better in the first round had won the Masters.

After all, it took 61 minutes after play began for the field to record the first birdie. Defending champion Tiger Woods was three over par after his first five holes en route to a four-over-par 76.

Northern Ireland's Darren Clarke was 'smokin' during the first round of the Masters Tournament.

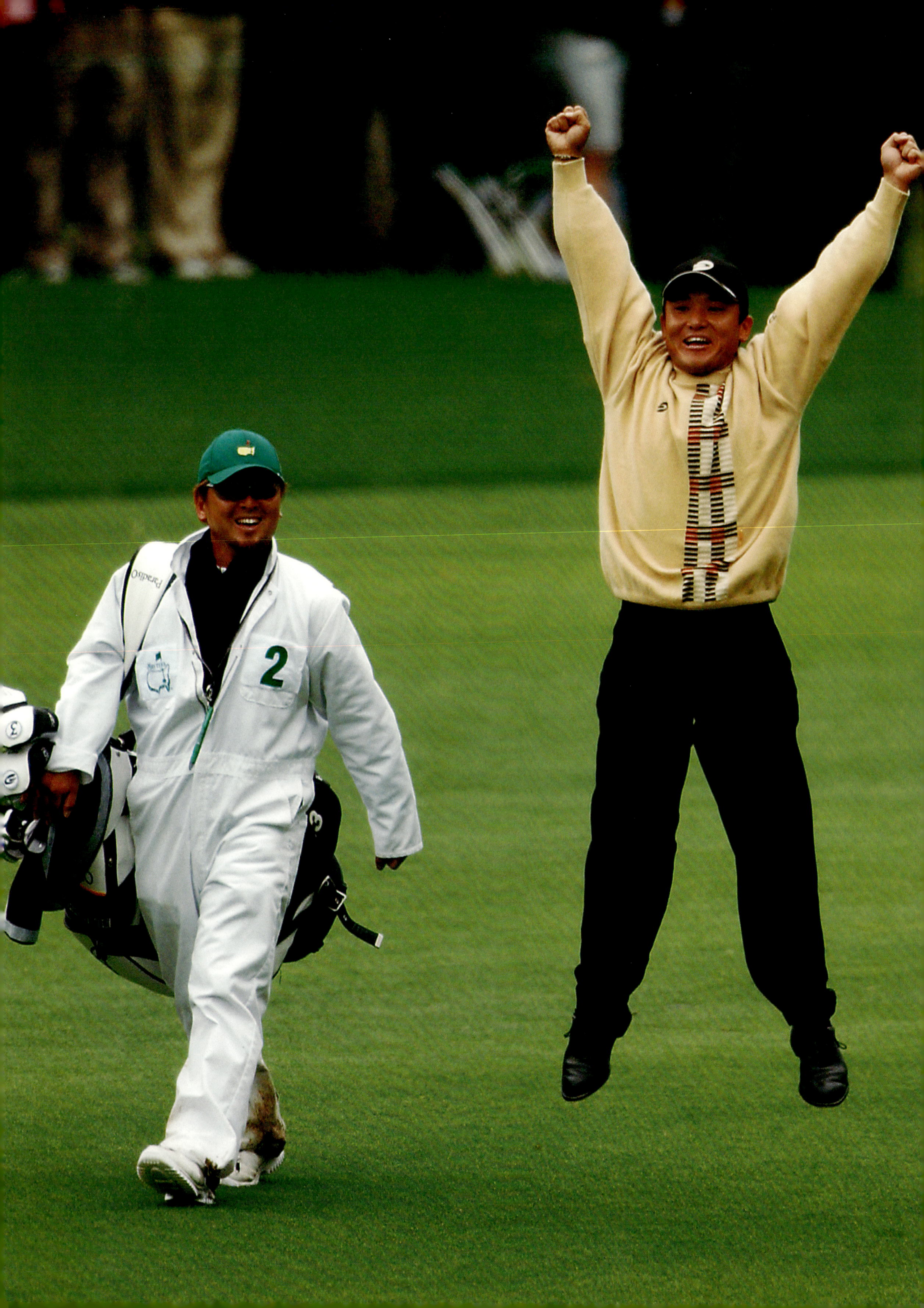
2

Early starters, who received the worst of the raw weather, suffered the most.

"The thing that made it really difficult was it was windy and cold," said Australian Stuart Appleby after an opening 77. "Anyone in the red (under par) will be a very happy man today."

"It's as difficult as I've seen in 15 or 16 years," said former PGA champion Jeff Sluman of the difficulty facing the field.

But leave it to the irrepressible Fuzzy Zoeller to add a dash of levity to a hard day's work.

How did the golf course play? Zoeller, the 1979 Masters champion, was asked.

"It's good," said Zoeller, tongue-in-cheek. "There are seven or eight par-5s out there."

Augusta National Golf Club has only four par fives but some long par fours played much longer, Zoeller surmised.

"Eighteen was a monster today," said Appleby, who played a two-iron second shot, came up short, and made a double bogey six. "My ego was smashed around by the golf course a bit. I've got to get back to a positive bit when I go out for the second round."

"The golf course played very, very difficult," said veteran Steve Lowery. "We're not used to playing this golf course that difficult."

Overall, the scoring average for the 93-player field finished at a whopping 76.203 strokes.

At the end of the morning round, few players were able to master the layout and some struggled mightily to navigate any part of it.

Among those were former champions Tom Watson (75), Mark O'Meara (76), Fuzzy Zoeller (77), Bernhard Langer (79), Gary Player (82), Arnold Palmer (83) and Jack Nicklaus (85).

Woods, hampered by an inability to make any timely putts, shot 76, his highest round as a professional in the Masters. He did not make a birdie.

"I didn't hit the ball all that bad," said Woods, "but I didn't make any putts. I had a couple of bad breaks." Woods found his ball in the bunker at No. 2, and a shot in a fairway depression at No. 5. He made par and bogey respectively.

But the day belonged to the burly 34-year-old Clarke, who was making his sixth start in the event and owns a tie for eighth in 1998 as his best finish.

Five birdies, an eagle at the 500-yard, par-5 15th when he sank a 25-foot putt, and a lone bogey at the 490-yard, par-4 11th hole via a three-putt, left the Irishman ahead of his peers.

"It's been solid all day," said the

(Opposite page): Japan's Shigeki Maruyama was leaping for joy after holing out his third shot for an eagle at the par-5 eighth hole during the first round. (Above left): Floodlights illuminated the practice tee for those early starters prior to the first round. (Above right): A Masters patron asked for quiet so that the players could work undisturbed during the opening round.

18-HOLE
LEADERS

D. Clarke	66
R. Barnes	69
S. Garcia	69
M. Weir	70
N. Price	70
D. Toms	71
T. Taniguchi	71
J. Maggert	72
P. Lawrie	72
J. Kelly	72
T. Clark	72

2003 MASTERS • AUGUSTA NATIONAL GOLF CLUB

What They're Writing

Once again that old adage was proven true yesterday: The Masters begins with a marathon on Friday.

OK, you've never heard that one before. Then again, much of what transpired on the first day of competition in the 67th Masters you haven't seen at this most precious of golf's major championships.

Begin with officials trying to squeeze the opening two rounds into one day for the first time in history, then consider that rounds were contested at an excruciatingly slow six-hour pace, and ponder further the opening 76 posted by overwhelming favorite and two-time defending champion Tiger Woods -- his worst score as a pro here -- and the surprising play of US Amateur champ Ricky Barnes.

Throw that all into a mix with a 7,290-yard golf course that played more like 7,600 after five straight days of rain, and you had a start to the Masters unlike any in history.

- Jim McCabe
Boston Globe

Darren Clarke didn't seem all that impressed with the extraordinary round of 66 he somehow managed to shoot Friday morning after the rain finally moved out of northeast Georgia.

He called it "solid," even though it resulted in the largest lead (three shots) after the first round of the Masters since 1982, when Jack Nicklaus held that edge over Jack Renner and Fuzzy Zoeller. And he had become the first player from Ireland to ever lead the Masters.

"I've been hanging in there," the big Irishman said. "I'm not far off from my best round."

Maybe it was the reason that caused him to temper his enthusiasm or maybe it was the knowledge that another round over Augusta National Golf Club awaited him after a quick sandwich.

When asked if he was glad to get to play another 18, he patted his stomach and said, "Does it look like it?"

- Mike Dudurich
Pittsburgh Tribune-Review

Tiger Woods went birdieless for the first time in 31 career Masters rounds, and he lost to an amateur by seven strokes. Jack Nicklaus went birdieless to shoot his worst score in 158 career Masters rounds.

Let's just say it was that kind of day at Augusta National Golf Club on Friday. And that was only the half of it – which for a few select favorites was a good thing.

They played wall-to-wall golf, from sunup to sundown, in a 12-hour marathon that could be described only as brutal.

- Scott Michaux
Augusta Chronicle

(Left): Spain's Sergio Garcia celebrates one of his five first round birdies.
(Opposite page - top): Jack Nicklaus, getting his putter from son Jack Nicklaus II, right, was a familiar sight during first round play.
(Bottom): South African Ernie Els kept his gaze on this pitch shot during first round play Friday.

FIRST ROUND SCORING

ROUNDS	93
BELOW 70	3
BELOW PAR	7
PAR	4
OVER PAR	82
80+	15
SCORING AVG.	76.204
LOW SCORE	D. CLARKE, 66
HIGH SCORE	T. AARON, 92

2003 MASTERS • AUGUSTA NATIONAL GOLF CLUB

(Above): Defending champion Tiger Woods escapes from one of Augusta National Golf Club's 44 bunkers. (Opposite page): Canadian Mike Weir, top, was ready for his putt during the first round while Darren Clarke waved to the patrons after another birdie.

6-foot-2, 225-pound Clarke, a nine-time winner on the PGA European Tour.

"I made very few mistakes and played well all day."

Barnes, a native of Stockton, Calif., and a senior at the University of Arizona, showed Woods a little of his long-driving talents.

The 22-year-old made five birdies and two bogeys. He hit 6-iron and pitching wedge to one foot at the second and seventh holes respectively. He missed the green right of the par-5 eighth with his third shot and after pitching on with his fourth missed a 10-footer for par to make his one bogey on the first nine. A birdie from eight feet at the 13th and a three-putt bogey from 75 feet at the 170-yard, par-3 16th set the stage for a fabulous finish.

Barnes hit a pitching wedge to 30 feet at No. 17 and a 6-iron from the right trees at No 18 to 7 feet and made both putts for birdies to tie Garcia.

"I'd take a 69 every round and take my chances," said Barnes, the 2002 U.S. Amateur Champion.

"I hope I come out and just play solid (in the second round)."

Garcia, only 23 himself, was blistering the course before stumbling at the end. Starting at No. 10, he chipped in for par at the 490-yard, par-4 11th hole and it kick-started a string of four birdies in the next five holes. He birdied the two par 5s - the 13th and 15th - with two putts from 45 feet and a sparkling up-and-down from the bunker and a three-foot putt. A nine-iron to four feet and a six-iron to three feet at the devilish 12th and 16th holes gave Garcia an opening nine total of 32.

A two-putt birdie from 20 feet at the 575-yard second hole, thanks to a sparkling 5-iron, left Garcia five under par and tied with Clarke at the time. But bogeys at Nos. 7 and 9 came when the Spaniard missed the greens with a nine-iron and seven-iron respectively, giving him a closing nine score of 1-over-par 37.

Despite the tough finish Garcia said he "felt good" about the first round.

"I missed about three drives that cost me," said the fifth year pro.

So a day that began with tough conditions left a few people satisfied with their first round but many hoping better things lie ahead in the second round.

"Maybe," said Appleby reflectively, "it is an advantage to play two (rounds). You can get into the second round and get something going."

What They're Writing
(continued)

Todd Galley surveyed the beauty around the 12th and 13th holes of Augusta National Golf Club on Friday and commented to his girlfriend, Deirdre Duval, that it would be a nice place for a marriage proposal.

Believing that Galley was speaking rhetorically, Duval agreed and continued watching her brother, David, walk down the 13th fairway after his tee shot during the first round of the Masters Tournament.

Then, to her surprise, Galley went to one knee in the cold mud, produced a diamond ring and proposed. When the shock wore off, she accepted.

"I thought he was just talking in general about what a beautiful spot it was," Duval said after receiving hugs and congratulations from several friends who watched Galley's proposal from a distance.

"Then he gets down on one knee, and then I thought he was just kidding. He's always kidding. But he wasn't, this time."

- Garry Smits
Florida Times-Union

The kid is not stagestruck.

Ricky Barnes might be at the Masters, instead of watching it on TV with his roommates at the University of Arizona, the way he has the last three years.

And the guy playing alongside him might be Tiger Woods, instead of just another college senior whose monthly living expenses don't equal Woods' cleaning bill.

And judging by the scores, Augusta National might be playing longer and tougher than it has at any time in the last 15 years.

But the kid does not scare easily.

"If you come out here ready to settle for a missed cut or something like that," Barnes said, "you're out here for the wrong reason."

- Jim Litke
Associated Press

Forget what you have read or heard elsewhere. A lower-seeded team beating a higher-seeded team in the NHL playoffs is not an upset.

If it were, the lower seeds would not have posted a 7-1 record in series openers. No, this is your upset: Tiger Woods played 21 holes at Augusta National without making a birdie.

Woods has won the past two Masters, increasing his victory total here in six pro starts to three. He had a streak of 10 consecutive under-par rounds that totaled 35 strokes under National's par.

Going back to his victorious Masters' pro debut in 1997, Woods had played 24 rounds at National: 10 in the 60s, five 70s, two 71s, five 72s and only two rounds over par (both 75s).

- Patrick Reusse
Minneapolis Star-Tribune

2003 MASTERS • AUGUSTA NATIONAL GOLF CLUB

Did You Know?

- When 2002 champion Tiger Woods did not make a birdie in the first round, it marked the first time since the third round of the 1999 British Open.

- You would think that when only three sub-70 rounds were recorded in the first round, it would mark a record-breaking day. But it didn't by a long shot. Four times since the Masters Tournament began in 1934 no contestants have broken 70 during the first round. Those years included 1934, 1936, 1954 and 1957.

- When Korea's K.J. Choi started birdie-birdie-birdie, it marked the quickest start by a first-time Masters participant since Milon Marusic in 1953.

- Amateur Ryan Moore holed out his third shot for eagle at the par-5 13th. That marked the first eagle by an amateur since Danny Green at the par-4 ninth hole in 2000.

- Since Ben Crenshaw was the last player to have the first round lead and win in 1984, three 18-hole leaders have finished runner-up. Those include Davis Love III in 1999, Fred Couples in 1998 and Greg Norman in 1996. One hundred players have held the first round lead but only 14 of those have gone on to win.

- Darren Clarke's lead of three strokes is the largest first round lead at the Masters since 1992 when Jeff Sluman and Lanny Wadkins led four players by three stokes (65-68).

2003 MASTERS • AUGUSTA NATIONAL GOLF CLUB

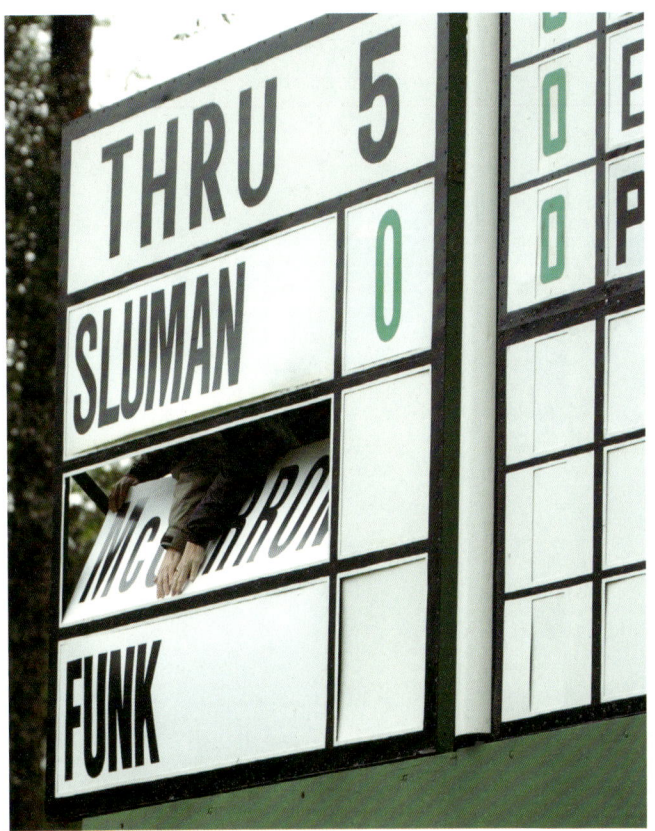

(Opposite page-top): Collegian Ryan Moore of Puyallup, WA., was one of five amateurs in the field (Opposite page-bottom): Masters patrons eagerly soaked in the atmosphere of first round play. (Left): Left-hander Phil Mickelson manufactured a deft escape from a bunker during his round of 73. (Above): Masters Tournament volunteers constantly keep patrons advised of how players are doing via manual scoreboards around the golf course.

STAT LEADERS

DRIVING DISTANCE	H. Mahan, 294 yards
DRIVING ACCURACY	C. Parry, J. Maggert, T. Clark, 14 of 14 fairways
GREENS IN REGULATION	R. Beem, 15 of 18
TOTAL PUTTS	P. Lawrie, 23

THE LEADERS' CARDS

PAR	4	5	4	3	4	3	4	5	4	36	4	4	3	5	4	5	3	4	4	36	72
D. CLARKE	(3)	5	(3)	3	4	3	4	5	4	34	(3)	[5]	3	(4)	(3)	(3)	3	4	4	32	66
R. BARNES	4	(4)	4	3	4	3	(3)	[6]	4	35	4	4	3	(4)	4	5	[4]	(3)	(3)	34	69
S. GARCIA	4	(4)	4	3	4	3	[5]	5	[5]	37	4	4	(2)	(4)	4	(4)	(2)	4	4	32	69
M. WEIR	4	(4)	4	3	4	3	4	5	(3)	34	4	4	3	(4)	4	5	3	4	[5]	36	70
N. PRICE	4	(4)	(3)	[4]	[5]	(2)	(3)	5	4	34	4	4	3	5	4	5	3	4	4	36	70
D. TOMS	4	5	[5]	[4]	(3)	(2)	4	[6]	[5]	38	4	[5]	(2)	(4)	(3)	(4)	3	4	4	33	71
T. TANIGUCHI	4	(4)	(3)	3	4	[4]	4	5	4	35	[5]	4	3	5	[5]	(4)	3	(3)	4	36	71

○ Eagle ○ Birdie □ Bogey ▢ Dbl Bogey or higher

(Above): A brightly dressed Tom Lehman took a mighty swing at this shot in his first round. (Left): Former champion Jose Maria Olazabal studied his putt during the first round. (Opposite page): Ricky Barnes enjoyed his first official Masters round with a sparkling 3-under-par 69.

MICKELSON'S QUICK START PROVIDES SUCCESS

Over the course of the last three Masters, Phil Mickelson has enjoyed unparalleled success short of winning and 2003 was no different. Why? It's in his first round numbers.

Mickelson has started quickly at Augusta National Golf Club and generally remained consistent with his scoring since 2001 when he began a string of two third places finishes heading into the 2003 tournament.

Beginning in 2001, Mickelson has posted rounds of 67, 69 and 73, the latter under cold, harsh conditions in 2003. In those three first rounds, the left-handed golfer has averaged 4.66 birdies and only 2.33 bogeys per round.

Mickelson has hit 29 of 42 fairways and 35 of 54 greens in regulation in his first round scoring average of 69.66 strokes. Mostly, however, the talented Mickelson has averaged 27.33 putts per round to challenge for the Masters Tournament title.

A HEADY MASTERS START
Barnes Shoots Sparkling 69

He carries the blonde hair not unlike a former Masters champion of years ago.

Like Jack Nicklaus, amateur Ricky Barnes of Stockton, Calif., can hit a golf ball a long way just like the Golden Bear did in his youth.

The parallels between the two are striking. Both are big men. Nicklaus is 5-foot-11 and was over 200 pounds when he joined professional golf in 1962. Barnes is 6-foot-1, 200 pounds and his professional days still lie ahead.

But when Barnes came to his first Masters, he, like Nicklaus, had the opportunity of a lifetime and he faced the challenge head on.

And he made the golf world sit up and take notice with a 3-under-par 69 which left him tied for second with Sergio Garcia and only one of three players posting sub-70 scores in the opening round.

For the reigning U.S. Amateur champion it was a well-deserved moment in the national spotlight while playing alongside defending champion Tiger Woods and Argentina's Angel Cabrera.

"Having a little success in golf always makes you want to pursue a sport," said the University of Arizona senior who also played soccer and other sports in high school before settling solely on golf.

"Golf became serious once you start getting recruited about your junior year and then you kind of give up the rest of the sports. You get a scholarship in college."

There is, however, a difference between playing collegiate golf and playing in the Masters.

Barnes knew it right from the moment his invitation arrived from the Masters Tournament.

U.S. Amateur champions are traditionally paired with the defending Masters champion and this year that meant a 36-hole date with the world's No. 1 player.

That's enough to bring out the nerves.

"I don't think I had any nightmares about it," said Barnes, 22, the son of a former National Football League punter and a former schoolteacher.

"I am playing in the Masters. Not too many people can say that. My main concern going into the round was just the first tee shot. I wanted to put it in the fairway. I knew that was when I was going to be the most nervous."

Barnes was exactly right. His first shot in the 67th Masters hooked left into the trees of the par-4 first hole.

Woods calmed the youngster, telling him to relax and enjoy it.

That was all Barnes needed to hear.

"Ricky's a good kid," said Woods, himself only 27.

"He's a lot of fun. We had a good time out there and he was not only playing well, he was conducting himself the way he should."

Barnes made five birdies and two bogeys.

"I had two bogeys but I responded with birdies after that. Things are going really well. But if you told me I'd shoot 3-under-par, I run with it. I'm happy with the way I performed."

A frequent contender at the Masters was also impressed with Barnes' first round.

"He hits the ball a long way," said Phil Mickelson of Barnes' game.

"He's a very complete player. I wouldn't be surprised if he stays there for 72 holes."

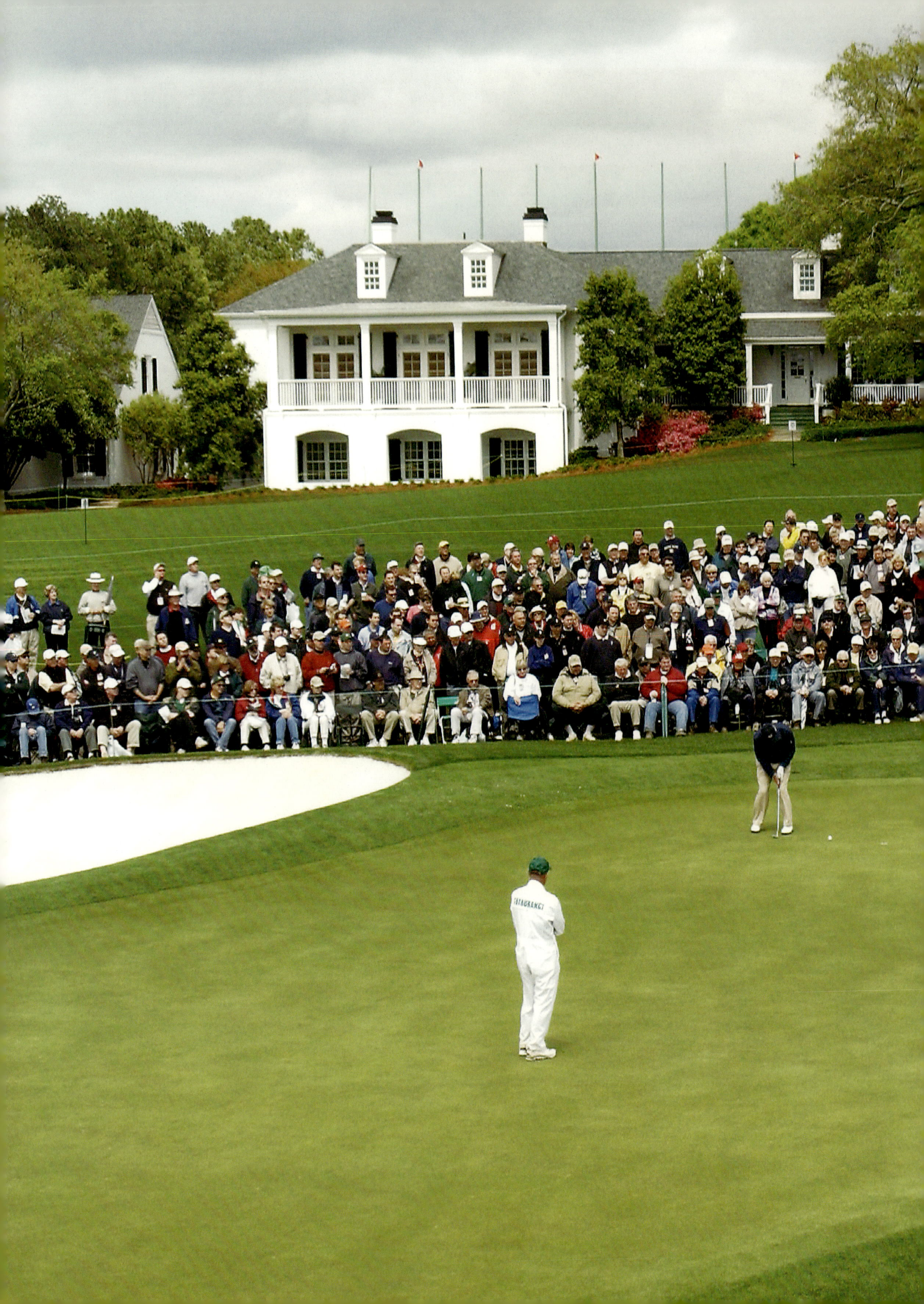

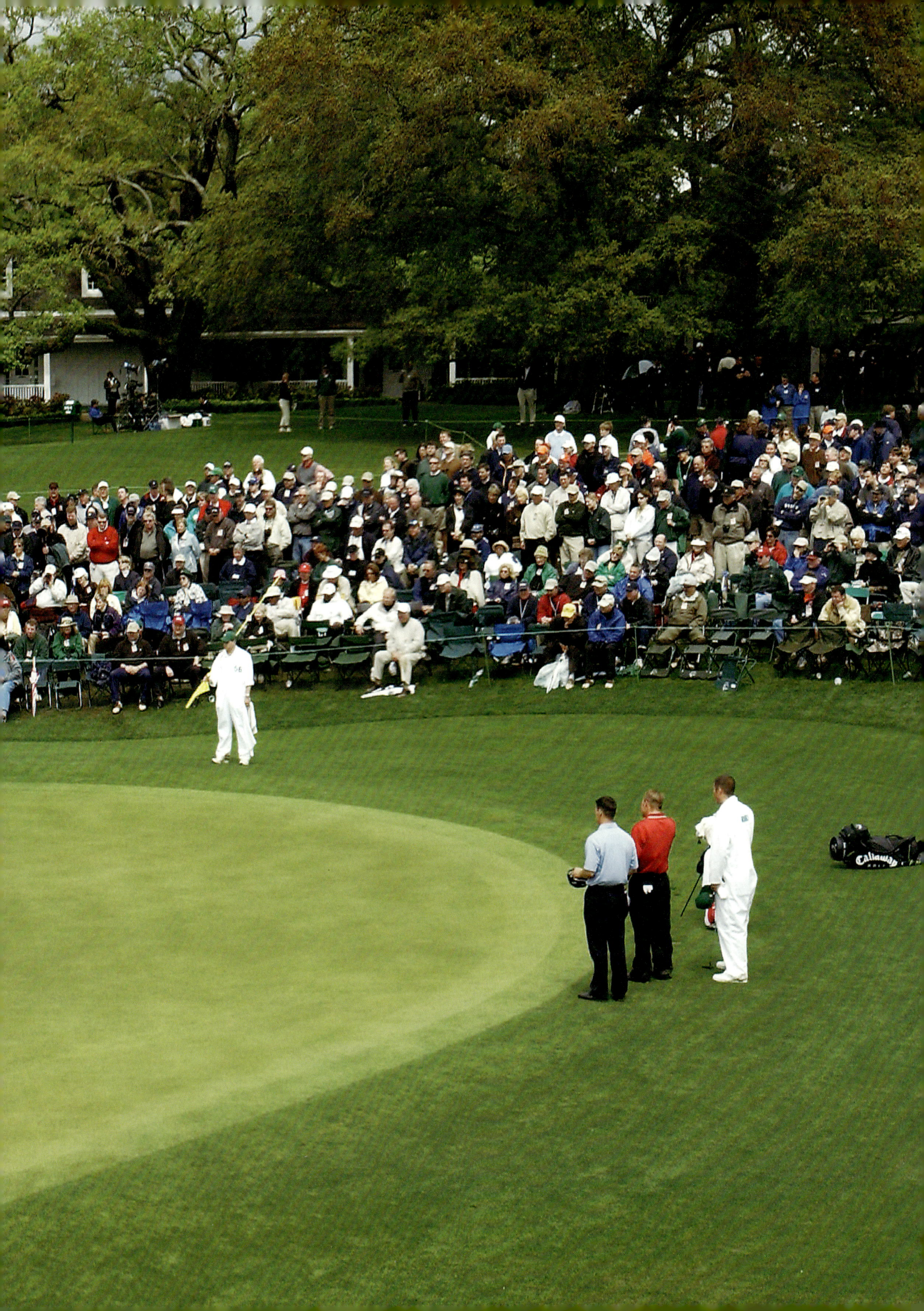
Callaway

Mike Weir, left, and caddie Brennan Little double check yardages during his second round 68.

ROUND TWO 2003

Weir's Mental Strength Provides Masters Edge

The Canadian believes mental toughness is the hardest part of leading.

The hardest thing, Mike Weir will tell you, is keeping your focus during a long day at the office. It doesn't matter, said Weir, whether you're an accountant, a banker or someone trying to win the Masters.

The Masters requires the ultimate in concentration and focus. Make one mistake, any player in the field will tell you, and disaster lurks around every corner of the Augusta National Golf Club course.

Leading the Tournament after 36 holes only brings that point sharply into focus.

"I knew this would be a tough challenge to stay with it mentally on a day like this," said Weir, who added a four-under-par 68 to an opening 70 for a 36 hole total of 138 as first and second round play was completed Saturday.

"I feel like my game has been very solid this year. My next step has been to contend in a major championship and I hope to do that."

The 32-year-old Canadian has not finished better than tied for 24th in three previous Masters appearances.

But he held a good-sized four stroke lead over Darren Clarke, the first round leader, and a five stroke lead over fellow left-hander Phil Mickelson, and U.S. Amateur champion Ricky Barnes. Clarke shot 76 in the carried over second round while Mickelson (70) and Barnes (74) kept themselves in red, under-par figures, too.

Only those four players finished two rounds in the rain-delayed Masters under par.

Five others were at even par 144, including former Masters champions Jose Maria Olazabal and Vijay Singh, but the 49 players who survived the 36-hole cut were all over the spectrum of scoring.

Although the field scoring average for round two dropped, the effect was small. The final tally for the 81 players finishing the second round was 1.553 strokes less than the opening round.

It took a 36-hole score of 5-over-par 149 or better to continue playing on the weekend.

Tiger Woods, for example, struggled when second round play concluded Saturday. He made a double bogey at the par-3 fourth hole, his third hole of the day, and played his last six holes in three over par. Woods needed a tough 3 footer on the par-4 ninth hole for par to make the cut and when his putt found the bottom of the hole, there was a welcome sigh of relief.

"When you miss some putts, it is hard to shoot a good number," said a disappointed Woods after a 73. "I hit some pretty poor shots this morning."

Woods, however, wasn't dismissing a chance to become the first man to win three Masters in a row.

"If I can get somewhere in the even par or under par by the end of the day I will be looking in pretty good shape."

Warmer overnight temperatures greeted those who needed to complete the second round and before most finished, the sun was warming competitors and patrons alike.

Weir, already a two-time winner on the PGA Tour leading up to the Masters but never a major championship winner, admitted completing the second round over parts of two days allowed for a great contrast in scoring conditions and scoring success.

"Early in the morning it was hard to get a feel," said the Ontario, Canada, native. "But my game felt like it was getting a little better as the week has gone on."

The temperature was in the 40s to start the second round April 11 and coupled with a slight wind and heavy fairways, getting a comfortable rhythm on the golf course was a big factor.

"I prepared myself for a long day and a long (golf) course," Weir said. "I told myself to not let myself slide mentally. And so I paid particular attention to that because it is easy when you get tired."

Weir's round included six birdies and two bogeys. His first nine and second nine were identical with three birdies and one bogey.

"You aren't going through this Tournament without any hiccups," said Weir, who made only one bogey in the first round.

"There are a lot of holes left."

Weir's play impressed his pursuers.

"That's great play, so to get that type of lead is impressive," said Mickelson of Weir's lead.

"His patience and demeanor, not just here but everywhere he plays, is situated perfectly (for Augusta National)."

Clarke, who required eight holes to finish his second round, struggled mightily to shoot 76 and trailed Weir by four strokes.

"I struggled a bit this morning, but I hung in there," said Clarke who restarted his round with a double bogey six at the par-4 11th hole, added a bogey at the par-5 15th and a birdie at the 17th

(Left): Three-time Masters champion Nick Faldo, and two-time winner Bernhard Langer, top, each hoped to add another Green Jacket. (Opposite page): Ricky Barnes watched the flight of his ball during the second round.

2003 MASTERS • AUGUSTA NATIONAL GOLF CLUB

hole for his second nine of 39.

"I have to give myself a pat on the back for shooting 76 - if you can do such a thing. There are momentum swings out there for everybody. Augusta doesn't give you anything."

Clarke's round included a rollercoaster scorecard. He made four birdies, six bogeys and one double bogey.

Mickelson's 70 and Barnes' 74 left them tied for third and full of hope.

Mickelson is still seeking his first major championship and Barnes' task is even greater. No amateur has ever won the Masters, although several, namely Billy Joe Patton, Ken Venturi, and Charles Coe have challenged in the final 18 holes during the 66 years of the event. Three of the five amateurs in 2003 made the 36-hole cut.

Mickelson, who required seven holes to finish his second round, said his 70 was satisfying.

"I thought if a guy is playing well, you could take advantage of it," he said of the double round.

But he warned that the rising temperatures and plethora of sunshine could drastically change the playing characteristics of the golf course the final two rounds.

"The last 36 holes the greens have dried out and it will play tougher," said Mickelson, predicting more tests ahead for the top players.

"I feel like there is a four or five under round and that can scoot you up the scoreboard."

Barnes' final eight holes included two birdies and two bogeys. His first 10 holes of the second round included a bogey, a birdie and a double bogey before play was suspended by darkness.

"I was kind of happy to shoot even par the last eight holes," said the collegian.

"I'm looking forward to a good weekend. Saturday is moving day so hopefully we will move up."

As the stage was set for the final two rounds, only 49 players have a chance to win the 2003 title.

One of them is Woods.

The Masters champion rules out nothing.

"The conditions are getting tougher which is good for the guys who are trying to make a move," Woods said.

36-HOLE
LEADERS

M. Weir	138
D. Clarke	142
R. Barnes	143
P. Mickelson	143
B. Faxon	144
P. Lawrie	144
J. Olazabal	144
V. Singh	144
D. Toms	144

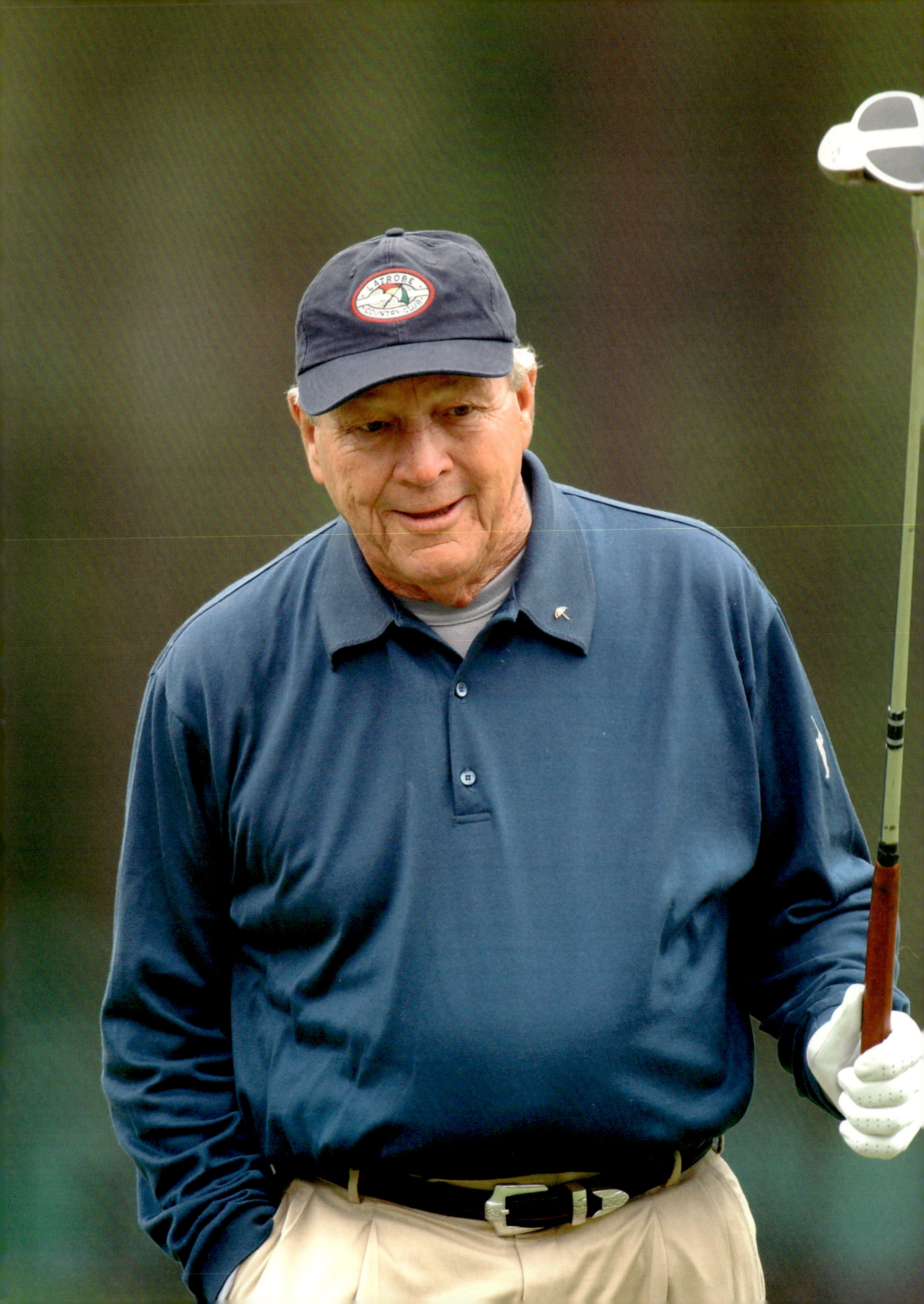
LATROBE
COUNTRY CLUB

(Opposite page): Arnold Palmer raises his putter in anticipation of a holed putt as he played the second round. (Above): Mike Weir, left, and past Master champion Tom Watson kept a keen eye on second round proceedings. (Below): England's most prized young player, Justin Rose, zeroes in on the hole location with this putt.

Did You Know?

- The four-stroke lead held by second round leader Mike Weir was the largest 36-hole lead at the Masters since Greg Norman held the same margin over Nick Faldo in 1996. The record for the largest 36-hole lead is five strokes by Harry Cooper in 1936, Herman Keiser in 1946, Jack Nicklaus in 1975 and Ray Floyd in 1976.

- Second round leader Mike Weir has never held the 36-hole lead in a PGA Tour event. He has held the first round lead twice and the third round lead five times. All five of his victories were in come-from behind fashion.

- In the previous 66 Masters Tournaments, 26 players who have either held or shared the second round lead have gone on to victory. The last player to do that was Jose Maria Olazabal, in 1999 who had a one stroke lead over Scott McCarron and then won his second Masters title by two strokes over Davis Love III.

- Ernie Els and Vijay Singh posted the first two bogey-free rounds of the Tournament in the second round. Els shot 66 and Singh shot 71.

2003 MASTERS • AUGUSTA NATIONAL GOLF CLUB

What They're Writing

He wanted to make history, but not this kind. After an opening-round 76, Tiger Woods was 10 strokes behind the leader, Darren Clarke.

No one has come back from 10 strokes behind after the first round to win the Masters, but that is what Woods will have to do if he is going to become the first golfer to win the event three consecutive years.

The former Cypress resident cut two strokes off his deficit during the darkness-shortened second round.

Woods played 11 holes of his second round and is 2-under par for that round, 2 over for the tournament, eight behind leader Mike Weir.

"I'm right where I need to be," Woods said. "I have a chance in the tournament."

Woods has erased similar deficits, though not in a major championship. In the 1998 Johnnie Walker Classic, Woods trailed Ernie Els by eight in the final round and won in a playoff.

- John Reger
Orange County Register

When the shutdown whistle sounded with people still scattered all over the course at 7:20 p.m. Friday, what was Tiger doing eight strokes behind Mike Weir.

And why had he been lurching around a full 10 strokes off the lead at one bleak point? Weird day all around.

By midday, when a brilliant sun started drying up the water-logged legend of a course, most of the bad jokes were worn out.

And, "These guys have to walk 8.3 miles just to finish 36 holes. They're going to need a ski-lift to take them up to the 18th green the second time."

The game was on at last after a rained-out Thursday.

The game Tiger and millions of Tigerites had been waiting for.

- Edwin Pope
Miami Herald

On a day when the Masters has never been crueler or more demanding, when the course played to an impossible length, Arnold Palmer was a resolute grinder.

He shot 83 in the rain-delayed first round and, when asked for an interview between rounds, said: "OK, but make it quick. I've got to take a nap." And his face crinkled into that familiar smile. He ate lunch, changed clothes, and came back out to tee it up again.

Just as he was the leader of Arnie's Army, which was first mustered on these grounds half a century ago, Arnold Palmer now leads The Gray Brigade.

- Bill Lyon
Philadelphia Inquirer

(Opposite page): Jack Nicklaus reacted with resignation to a missed second round putt. (Above): Sergio Garcia, right, and caddie Glen Murray were keenly focused on the task at hand.

THE LEADERS' CARDS

PAR	4	5	4	3	4	3	4	5	4	36	4	4	3	5	4	5	3	4	4	36	72	TOTAL
M. WEIR	4	④	3	3	5	3	4	④	4	34	4	5	3	④	③	④	3	4	4	34	68	138
D. CLARKE	5	④	4	4	5	3	③	④	5	37	5	6	3	5	4	6	3	③	4	39	76	142
R. BARNES	4	④	4	4	5	②	4	5	4	36	5	4	3	5	6	④	3	4	4	38	74	143
P. MICKELSON	③	5	③	②	③	3	4	5	4	32	5	4	4	④	4	④	5	4	4	38	70	143

◯ Eagle ○ Birdie □ Bogey ▢ Dbl Bogey or higher

2003 MASTERS • AUGUSTA NATIONAL GOLF CLUB

SECOND ROUND
SCORING

ROUNDS	92
BELOW 70	3
BELOW PAR	16
PAR	13
OVER PAR	63
80+	11
SCORING AVG.	74.650
LOW SCORE	E. Els, 66
HIGH SCORE	G. Zahringer, S. Ballesteros, 85

STAT LEADERS

DRIVING DISTANCE
P. Mickelson, 311 yards

DRIVING ACCURACY
J. Byrd, T. Byrum, 13 of 14 fairways

GREENS IN REGULATION
J. Furyk, 15 of 18

TOTAL PUTTS
M. Weir, J. Rollins, 22

(Right): Ernie Els reads the line of his putt during his second round that yielded the day's best score of 6-under-par 66.
(Opposite page): Arnold Palmer is surrounded by news media from around the world during his 49th Masters Tournament.

Casualties of the Cut

When the 36-hole cut came following the second round, a total of 14 former winners owning 28 titles were sent to the sidelines, but every champion from the last seven years still had a chance to win another title Sunday.

And 1992 Masters champion Fred Couples became the holder of the longest active player streak of consecutive cuts. Couples has made 19 straight in a streak which began in 1983. Two-time winner Bernhard Langer saw his consecutive cut streak stop at 19. Gary Player, however, holds the Masters record of consecutive cuts made with 23 from 1959-82.

Of the 16 first-time competitors in the Masters field, 11 made the cut, including three of five amateurs.

Those first-time competitors making the cut included amateurs Ricky Barnes, Hunter Mahan and Ryan Moore and professionals Rich Beem, Jonathan Byrd, K.J. Choi, Pat Perez, Chris Riley, John Rollins, Justin Rose and Phil Tataurangi.

The three amateurs making the cut were the most since four did so in 1999 and the second highest total in the prior 17 years.

The cut came at 5-over-par 149 with 49 players, including defending champion Tiger Woods, continuing on for the final 36 holes. Woods sank a 3 foot par putt on his last hole of the second round, the par-4 ninth, to make the cut on the number.

The 5-over-par total was the highest 36-hole aggregate since 1998.

Former champions missing the weekend action included Tommy Aaron, Seve Ballesteros, Charles Coody, Ben Crenshaw, Ray Floyd, Bernhard Langer, Sandy Lyle, Larry Mize, Jack Nicklaus, Arnold Palmer, Gary Player, Tom Watson, Ian Woosnam, and Fuzzy Zoeller.

The loss of Palmer, Player and Nicklaus was disheartening.

With a rain-soaked golf course and cold, windy weather facing them, golf's Big Three did not play their best during the first and second rounds.

At 73, Palmer was the fourth oldest Masters starter behind Fred McLeod who was 79 when he played in 1962, Doug Ford who was 78 when he played in 2001, and Jock Hutchison who was 75 in 1959. It was Palmer's 49th Masters appearance.

Nicklaus, 63, made his 43rd Masters start. Between Nicklaus and Palmer they have played 307 rounds and a total of 5,526 holes.

Player, a three-time winner who was celebrating the 25th anniversary of his last Masters win, made his 46th start and at 67 was the oldest international player in the field.

Nicklaus said he will take the decision to play at the Masters Tournament on a year-by-year basis. All former champions are given a lifetime exemption, but are asked to play only if they remain competitive and complete 36 holes.

Palmer acknowledged his goal is to play in 50 Masters' and that after 2004 his role may change.

Player just cherished his return to Augusta National Golf Club.

"It's always a thrill coming back and playing here," said the amicable South African. "The wonderful enthusiasm of the crowds is great. They gave me a standing ovation on every tee. The beauty of the golf course is unbelievable and, of course, the tradition is second to none."

Former champions who made the cut (total score in parenthesis)

* Jose Maria Olazabal (144)
* Vijay Singh (144)
* Nick Faldo (147)
* Mark O'Meara (147)
* Fred Couples (148)
* Tiger Woods (149)
* Craig Stadler (149)

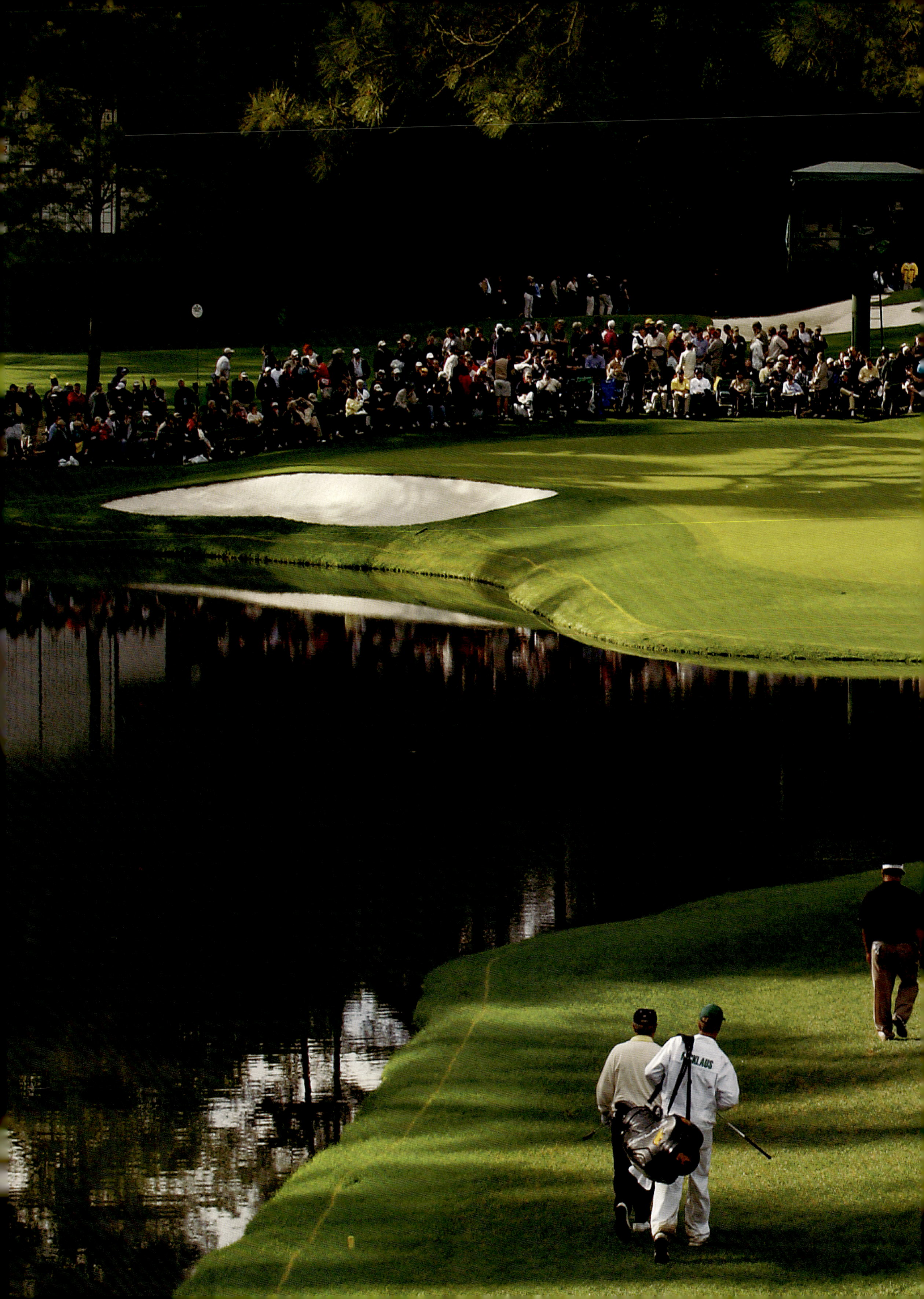

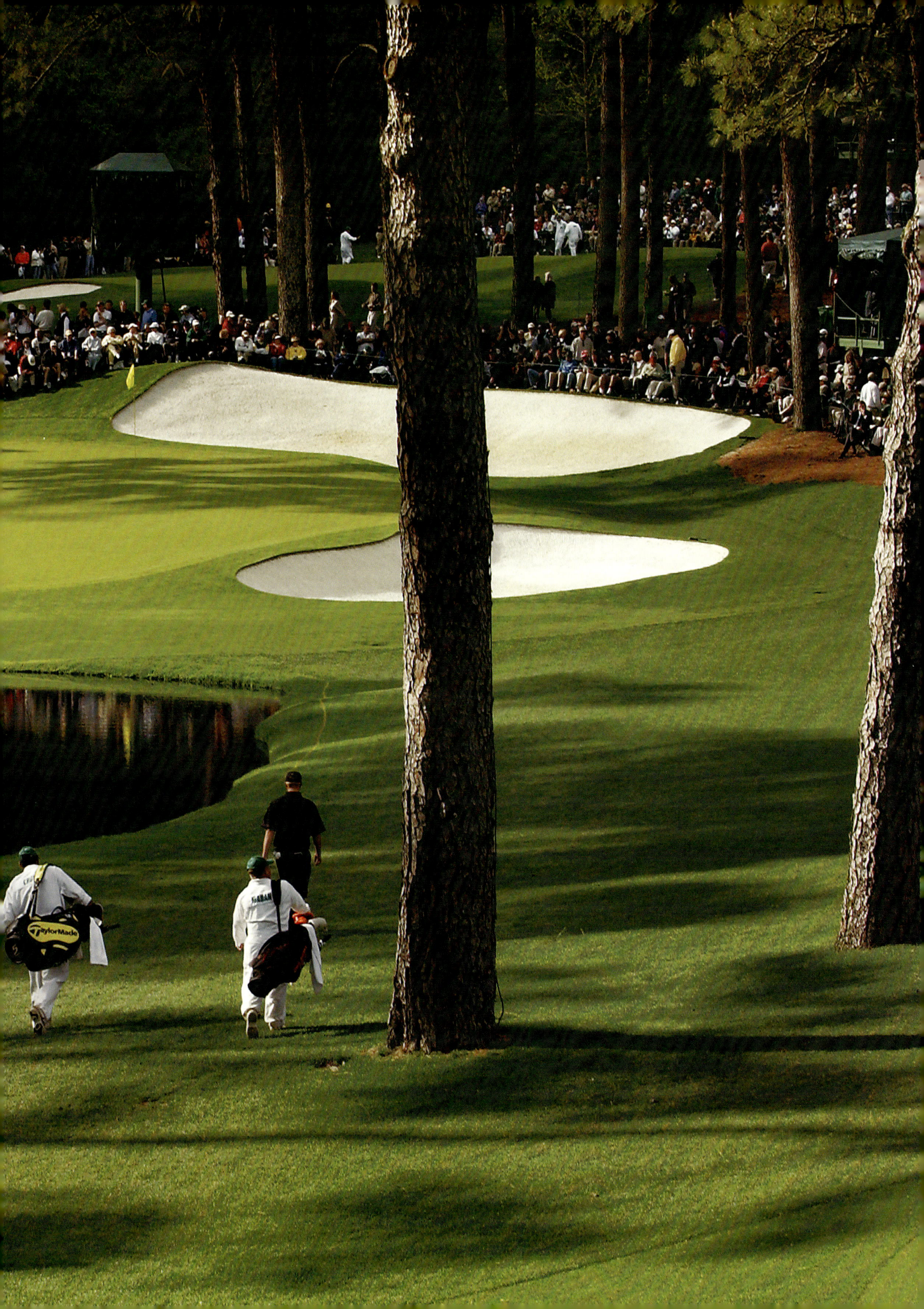
TaylorMade

ROUND THREE

Soft Spoken Maggert Efficiently In Control

Although he's been one of the game's top technicians, Jeff Maggert is looking for his first major championship.

If you ask around the world of professional golf, you'll find that Jeff Maggert has one of those most-envied swings. It's classic in style, one that will look the same for a lifetime, and one that is largely efficient.

It was just that efficiency that Maggert used to carve out a third round six-under-par 66 under temperatures in the 70s and sunny skies to take the 54-hole lead in the Masters.

Maggert, 39, assumed a two-stroke lead with his 5-under-par aggregate of 211 over Mike Weir who struggled with his iron play and shot 75 to rest at 213 heading into the final round.

Former Masters champion Vijay Singh and former PGA champion David Toms both added 2-under-par 70s and stood at 214. Defending champion Tiger Woods, who survived the 36-hole cut and jumped from a tie for 43rd when the round began to a tie for fifth, shot 66, two-time Masters champion Jose Maria Olazabal managed a 1-under-par 71 and Phil Mickelson shot 72. All three were at 1-under-par 215.

Those seven players were the only ones under par for the Tournament. Three more players were at even par and nine players stood within five shots of Maggert's lead. But those seven masterful performances were by and large the exception to the rule on a day deemed perfect for scoring.

After rains earlier in the week, the Augusta National Golf Club course began drying out under the warm, balmy spring breezes. That allowed for slight additional roll on tee shots, but it also allowed the undulating greens to dry. Challenging pin positions only added to the risk/reward of the day's play.

Maggert and Woods were the two major beneficiaries among the remaining players. Maggert, a resident of Houston, Tex., entered the Masters trying to re-energize his game. He was ranked 118th in the world and had won twice on the PGA Tour during his career. His last victory came four years ago in the WGC-Accenture Match Play Championship. Additionally, Maggert had recorded only six top-10 finishes in his last 61 starts. But the 66 was his lowest career Masters round.

Third round Masters leader Jeff Maggert hits his tee shot through a chute of trees at the uphill par-4 18th hole.

"I'm not known as a power hitter by any means," said Maggert, explaining how he managed five birdies in his final six holes despite the length of the 7,290-yard, par-72 layout, "so it was nice to see the ball roll a little bit and give myself an opportunity to hit a little bit of short irons into some of these holes."

"I still don't think you have to hit the ball 300 yards to shoot low scores here. A guy can manage his driver well and keep it in play and then you make your birdies hitting solid iron shots and good putts."

He survived a watery double-bogey at the par-4 11th hole, and saved par at the next hole before sprinting home in Herculean style.

"After 11 I was on the brink of collapse after making double bogey," said Maggert. "I hit a poor shot on 12 and saving par there gave me a bit of a boost. I tried to hit some good shots coming in."

An improved short game - something Maggert has needed as he struggled with his game over the last two years - was his savior until his strong finish.

"I didn't hit the ball (well) the first two rounds," he said of scores of 72 and 73, "but I hit the ball solid (Saturday) and it's nice to look up and see the ball going to the pin. It's something I've been working on and I feel very good about my short game and very good with the putter."

Maggert said all he did with his third round 66 was "give myself the opportunity" to win his first major championship.

"But Sunday is when it all happens," he said realistically.

Yes, Sunday is when the Masters separates the contenders from the pretenders.

The pressure of being in or near the lead of the Tournament can take its toll on even the best of them.

Weir, for example, held as much as a six-stroke lead early in the third round. He missed 10 of 18 greens in regulation before the day was over and finished four over par the final 10 holes to trail Maggert instead of lead him.

"It was a little bit disappointing," said Weir of his struggles. "I would have liked to play better than 75. My iron shots were off and they seemed to put me on the wrong side of the hole. But I'm still in the last group tomorrow and I still have a chance to win."

Two birdies and two bogeys on the first nine kept the Canadian on level terms with the scorecard but the second nine would be a difficult and sometimes harrowing story.

Weir ran through Amen Corner - hole Nos. 11-13 - with great difficulty.

His 5-iron second shot from 215 yards at the downhill 490-yard, par-4 11th embedded above the water hazard fronting the green. Using a pitching wedge, Weir exploded the ball onto the green and two-putted for a good bogey.

His 7-iron tee shot at the 155-yard 12th flew the green, brought up mud on the ball from the pitch mark, and forced Weir to stroke his second shot more forcefully to insure he didn't leave it short. He made a good par.

At No. 13, after turning his tee shot around the dogleg left, Weir chose a 3-iron for a shot where the ball was slightly below his feet.

"I had 215 yards plus the wind was going left-to-right," he said,

(Opposite page top): Phil Mickelson used his short-game excellence, particularly on the putting green, to stay in contention.
(Opposite page bottom): Jonathan Byrd pitching onto the green during the third round. (Above): A Masters Tournament volunteer kept track of the hole-by-hole numbers during play.

Did You Know?

- Ernie Els' eagle on No. 7 is the seventh on that hole. The last time No. 7 was eagled was by Larry Mize in 1999. For Els it was his eighth career eagle at the Masters. He also eagled No. 7 in the first round in 1997.

- Jeff Maggert's 66 was his career low Masters round. In 31 rounds, he has been in the 60s three times.

- Tiger Woods' 66 was the only bogey free third round score and Jeff Maggert's 211 is the highest 54-hole score since Ben Crenshaw led in 1989 with a 3-under-par 213.

- Seven players finished 54 holes with sub-par totals. That's the lowest number of players in the red since 1989 when three players were under par through three rounds - Ben Crenshaw (-3), Scott Hoch (-2) and Mike Reid (-2).

- The only first-time Masters competitor standing in the top-10 through 54 holes was Jonathan Byrd. Byrd recorded a third round score of 71 and was tied for eighth at even par 216.

replaying the shot. "I had a little bit of mud on the ball but I made a beautiful swing, made great contact. The ball was cutting right to the center of the green and probably the last 25 yards the ball drifted back to the right."

It found the tributary of Rae's Creek fronting the green of the 510-yard, par-5 hole and forced Weir to take a penalty stroke and drop. From there he made a bogey six.

"It seemed a perfect shape wind (for the shot) at the time," said Weir.

From there, Weir three-putted Nos. 16 and 17 to finish off his day.

He tried to keep an even keel mentally despite the rough finish.

"I didn't have much of a frustration level today," he said. "I wasn't far off of a good round, a 70 or 69."

Woods did emerge from two disappointing rounds and his climb up the leader board sent a murmur among Masters patrons.

It did make Maggert notice too.

"I felt Tiger would play a good round today," said Maggert of the world's No. 1 ranked player, "even though he struggled with his game and flirted with the cut."

"But there's nobody out there I can control tomorrow but myself."

Woods knew he needed to get back in the hunt and getting to even par at the end of the third round would put him back where he wanted to be.

Starting on No. 10, Woods made three birdies on his first nine holes.

"Good breaks were going my way," he said, "and I got a big break at 11."

Woods made a monster 50-foot putt for birdie that jump-started his round and sent his adrenaline level shooting upward.

Birdies at the two par 5s - Nos. 13 and 15 - gave the three-time Masters champion just the push he needed.

He birdied the par-5 second, holed a downhill 40-footer for a birdie deuce at the par-3 sixth, and ended his run up the leader board with a birdie at the short, par-4 seventh.

Sixty-six said his scorecard, pulling a big smile across his face.

"Most major championships I've either been tied for the lead or leading in the final round," said the winner of eight major championships, including all four Grand Slam events.

"Even though I'm four back, that is not inconceivable. It makes you feel assured because you've done it before."

2003 MASTERS • AUGUSTA NATIONAL GOLF CLUB

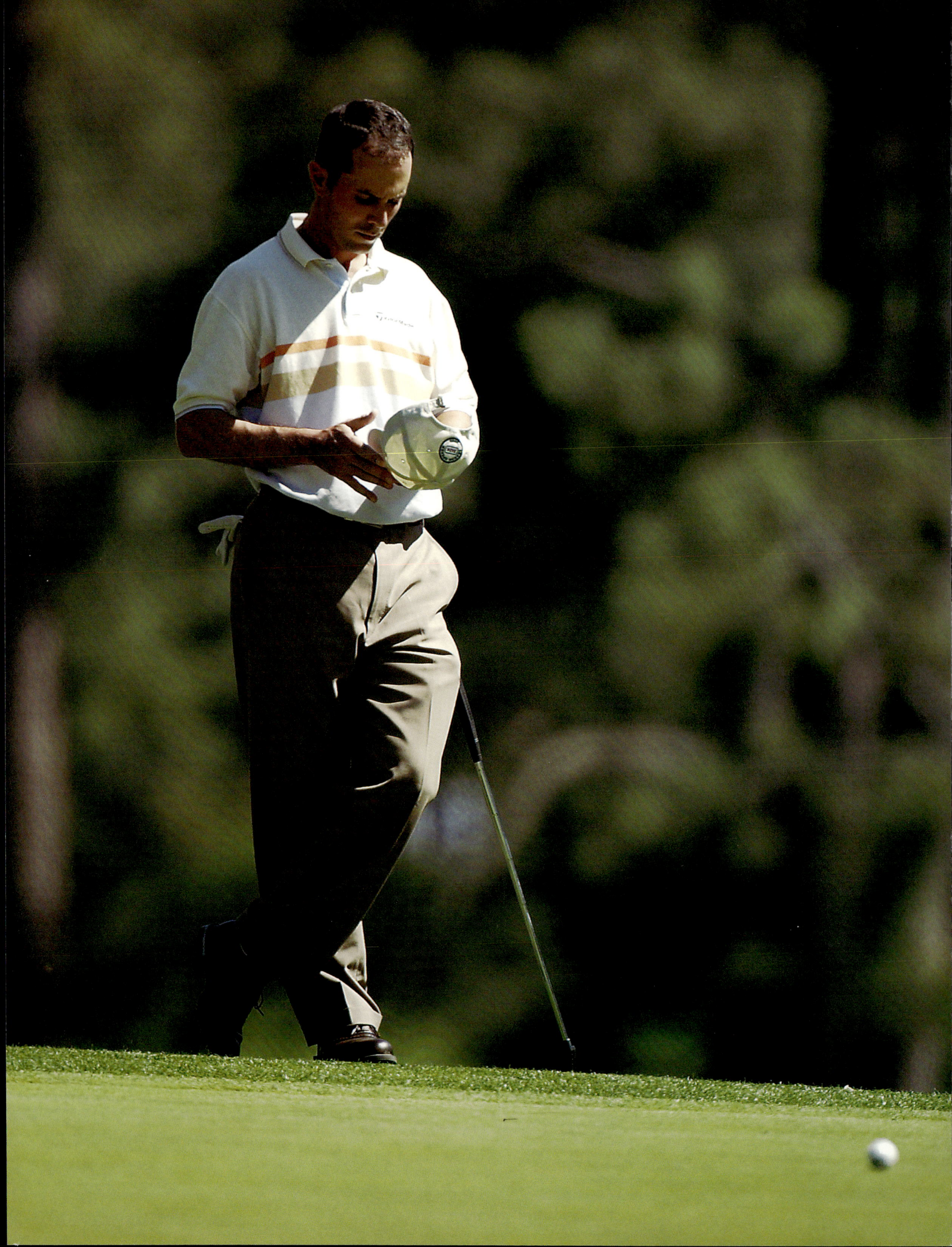

WILL FINAL PAIRING PROVIDE CHAMPION AGAIN?

Maybe it is just coincidence, but then maybe it's not.

If you are in the final pairing after three rounds of the Masters, the odds are good you will win a coveted Green Jacket.

After 54 holes of the 2003 event that meant that Jeff Maggert or Mike Weir would have the best shot at winning the title, judging from the past dozen tournaments.

Over the last 12 years every winner has come from the final twosome. Nick Faldo in 1990 was the last player to win the Masters without playing in the final group.

(Opposite page): Mike Weir during the third round. (Above left): Masters champion Jose Maria Olazabal scored a 71 in the third round. (Above): Amateur Ricky Barnes' iron game caused him to struggle with a third round 75.

2003 MASTERS • AUGUSTA NATIONAL GOLF CLUB

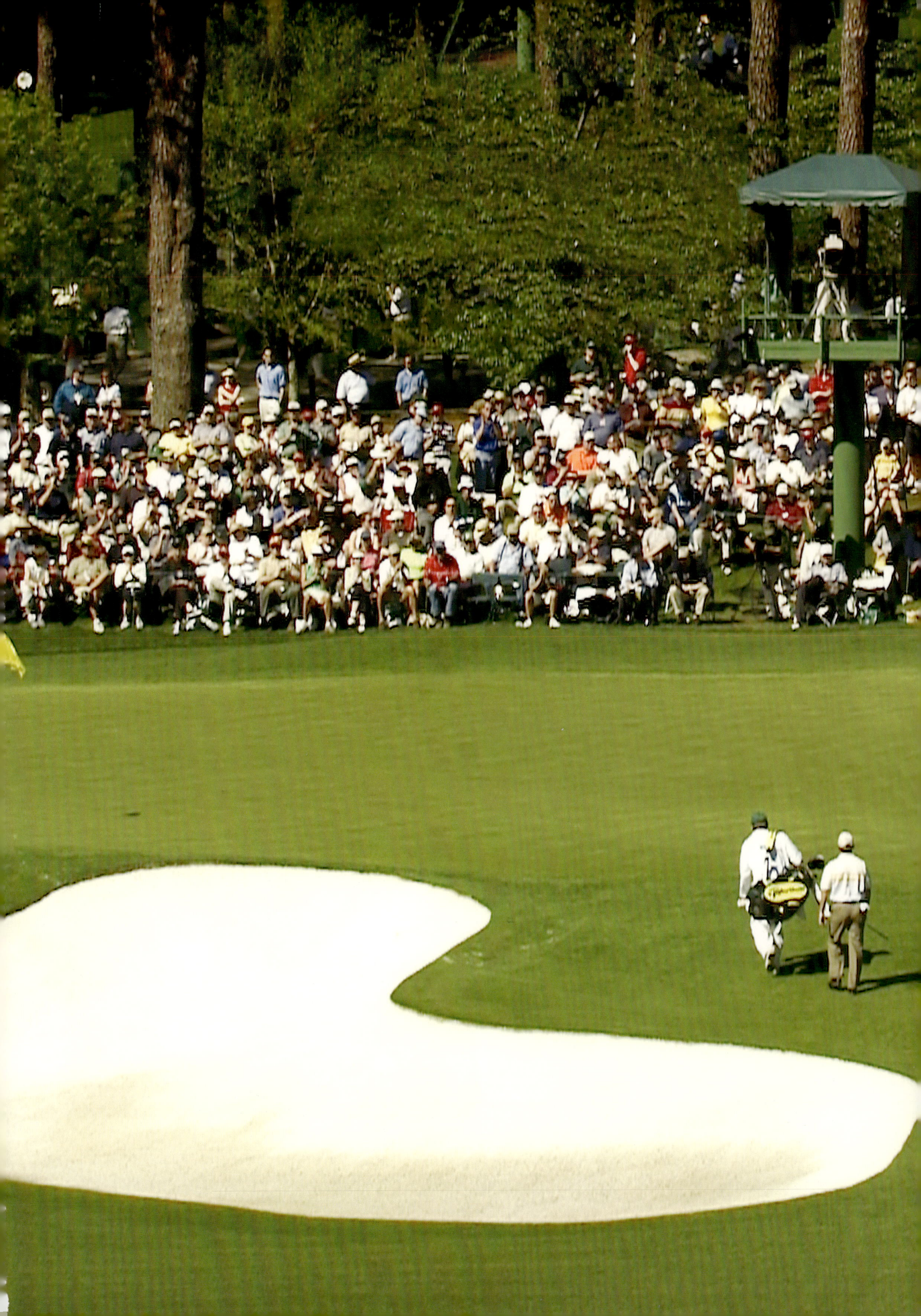

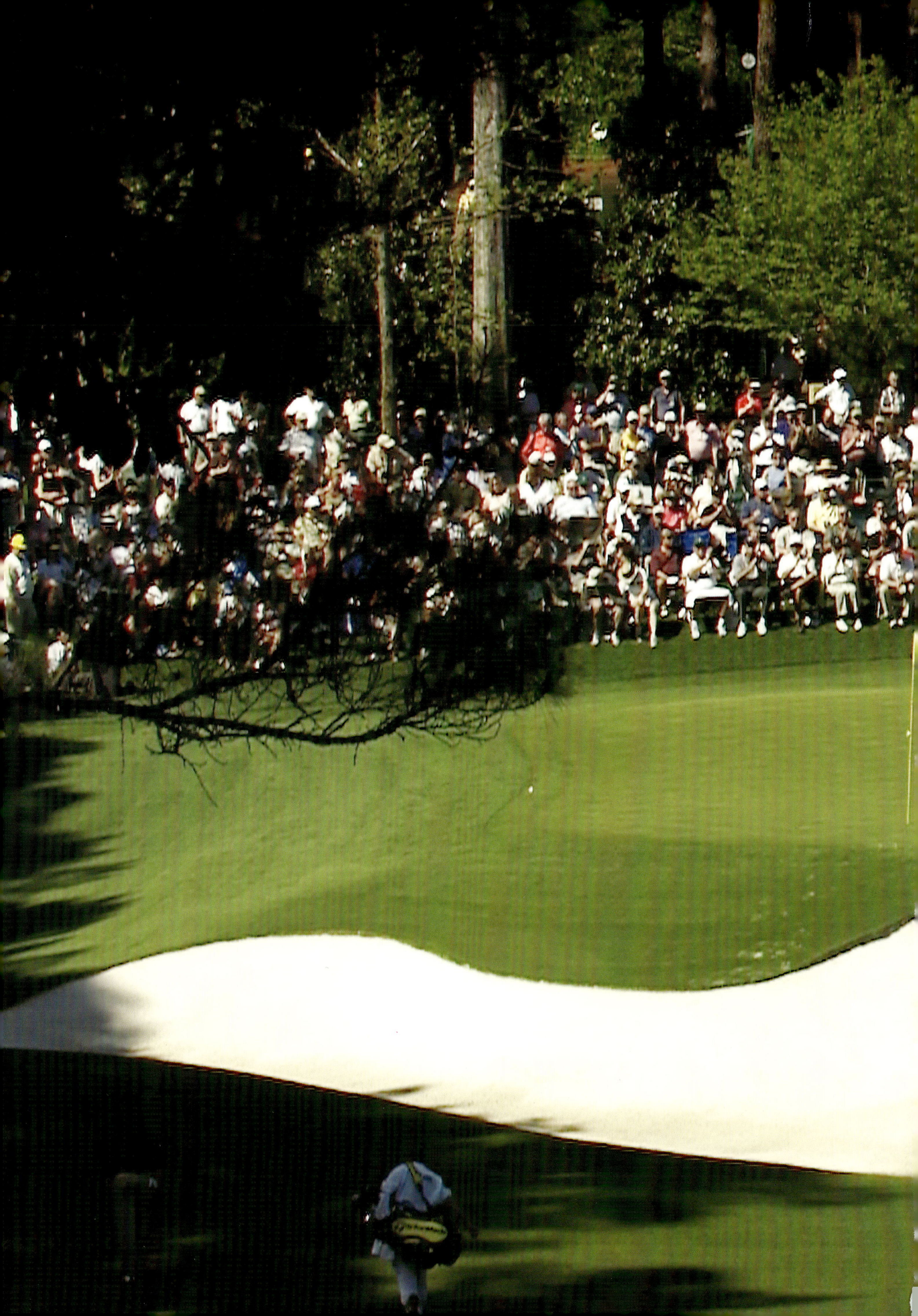

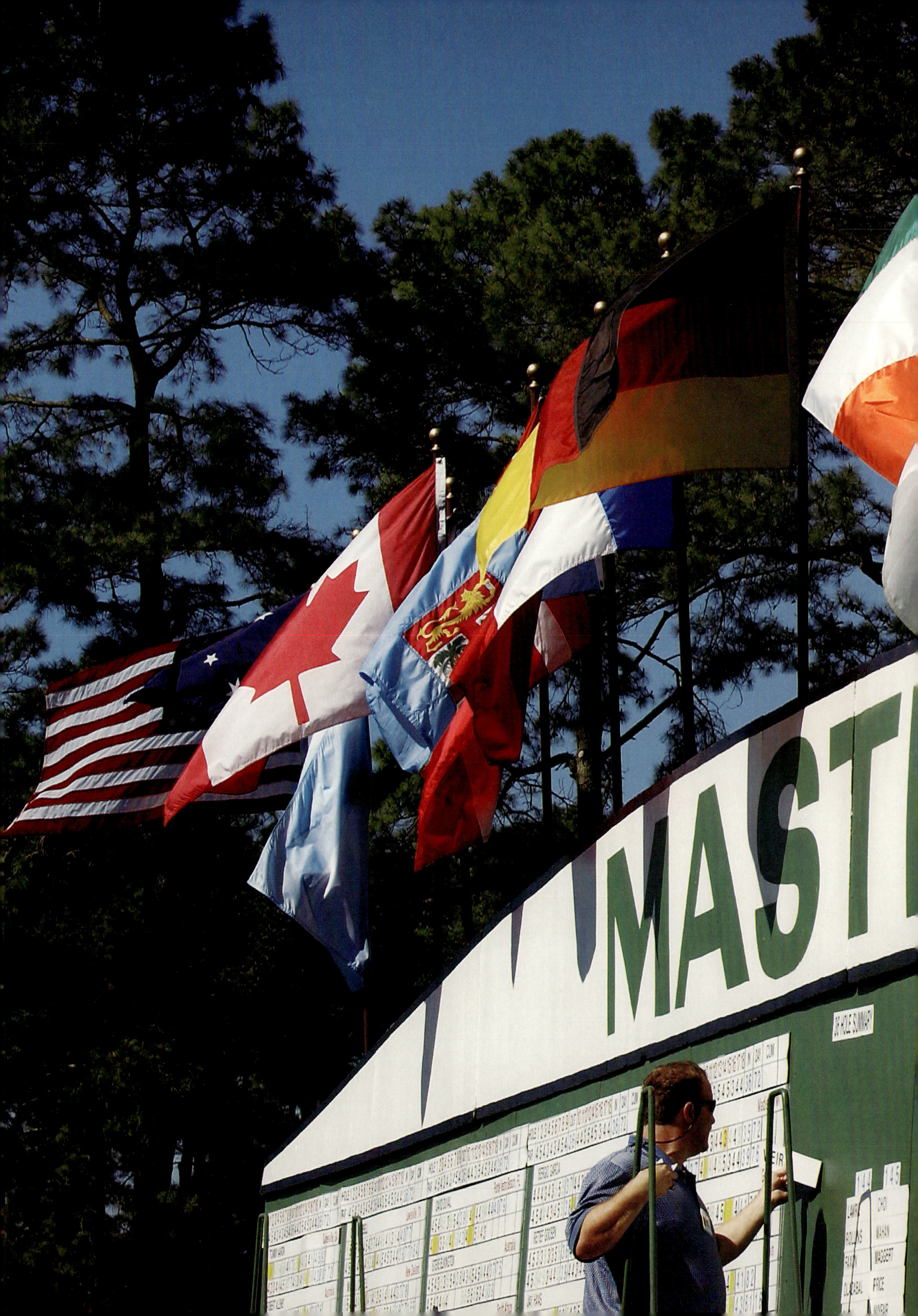
MAST

ERS
LOREN ROBERTS
Germantown, TN
Dunedin, FL
JOHN ROLLINS
Argentina
EDUARDO ROMERO
England
JUSTIN ROSE
Australia
North Palm Beach, FL
JACK NICKLAUS
Spain
JOSE MARIA OLAZABAL
Windermere, FL
MARK O'MEARA
Latrobe, PA
ARNOLD PALMER
The Woodlands, TX
McKinney, TX
Japan
Jacksonville, FL
PHIL TATAURANGI
DAVID TOMS
KIRK TRIPLETT
SCOTT VERPLANK
TOM WATSON

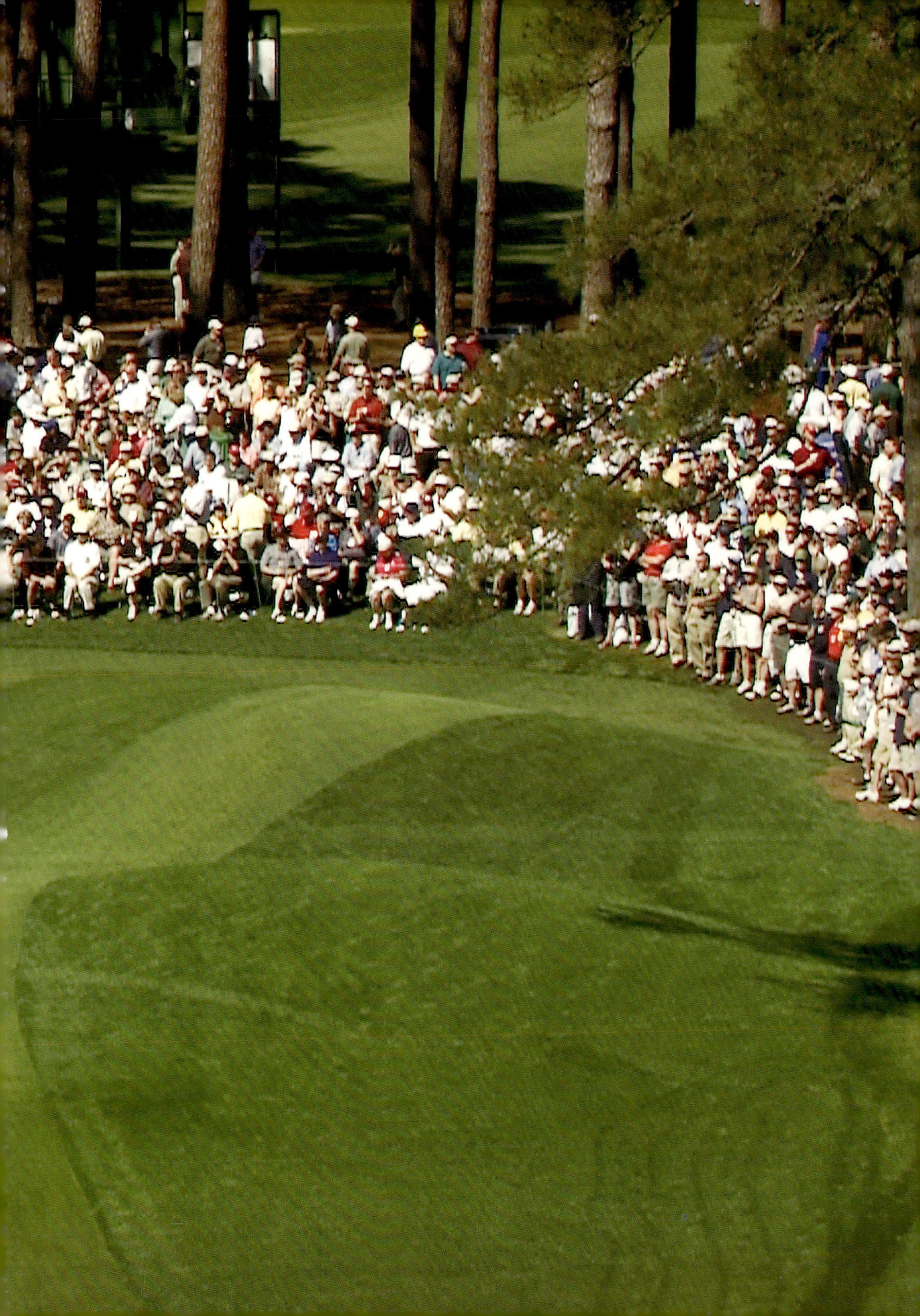

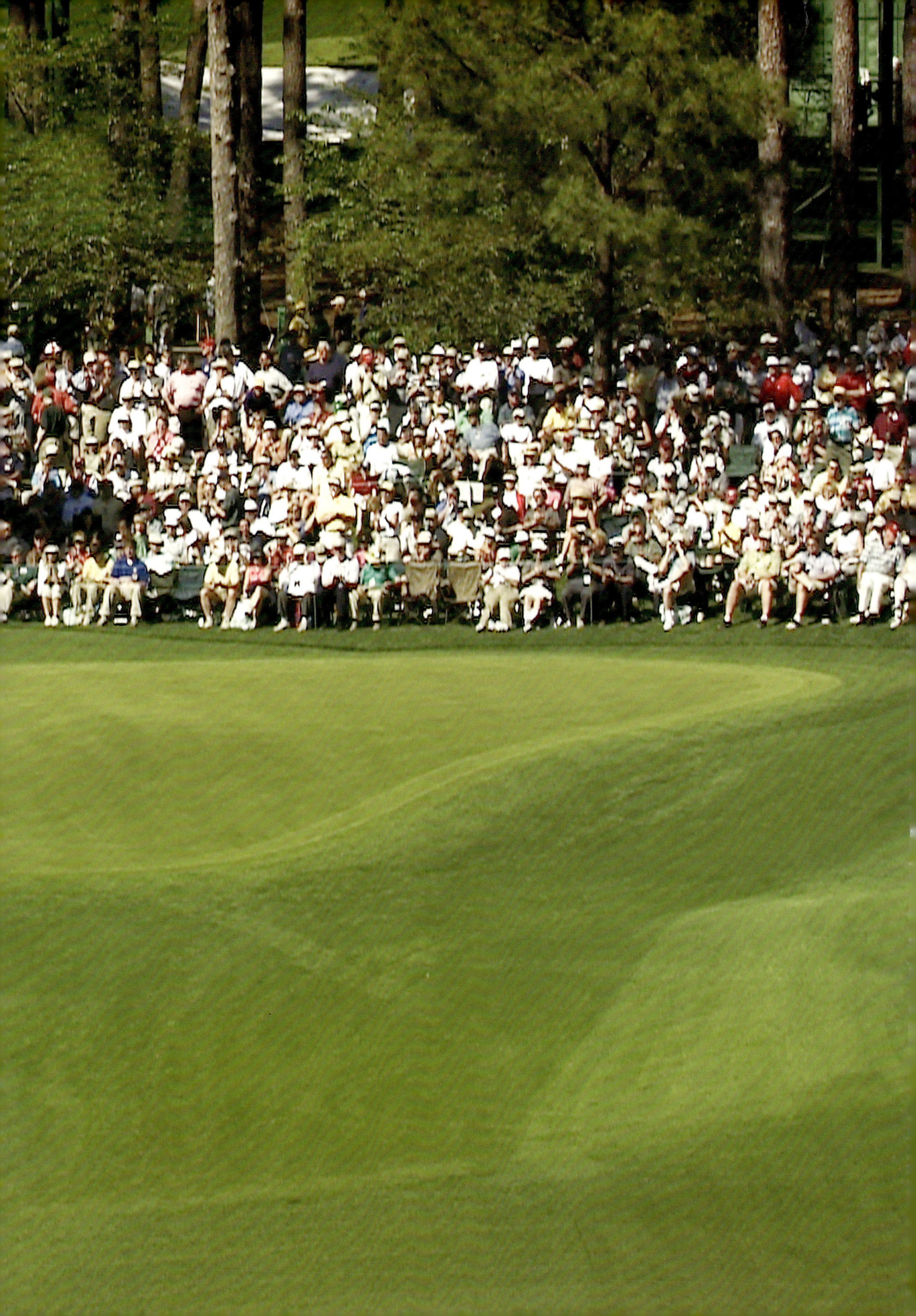

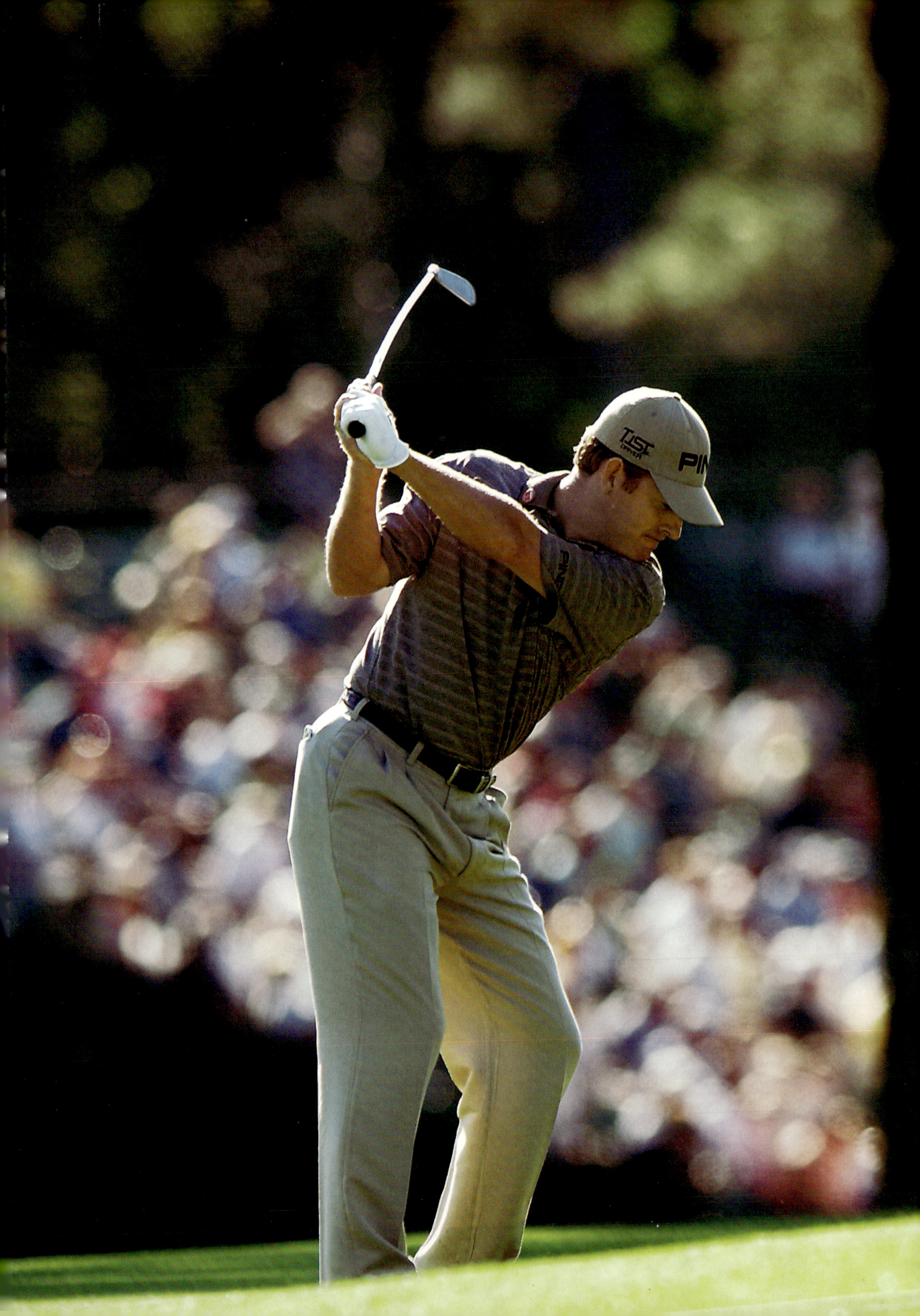

What They're Writing

The most lethal closer in golf history will get a chance to win his first major championship playing from behind today at Augusta National Golf Club. You have to figure he's ready. Saturday was a right fair dress rehearsal.

Tiger Woods shot 6-under-par 66 to soar from a tie for 43rd place to a tie for fifth. He goes into today's final round of the 67th Masters Tournament only four shots behind leader Jeff Maggert.

Once in mortal peril of missing the cut, Woods resuscitated his quest for a third consecutive green jacket.

— Phil Richards
Indianapolis Star

(Opposite page): Jeff Maggert was in fine third round form with a 6-under-par 66 and a 54-hole leading total of 211. (Top): Former champion Vijay Singh, shown pitching, made another strong run for a second Masters title. (Right bottom): A Masters Tournament marshall kept a lookout for players' shots from his station along the fairway.

2003 MASTERS • AUGUSTA NATIONAL GOLF CLUB

What They're Writing
(continued)

He is 39, and he has the chance of a golfing lifetime in front of him.

He is at the top of the leader board at the Masters, positioned -- and judging by his demeanor, poised -- to play in the final group of the last round. He is at the cusp of a major championship of monumental proportions.

He is Jeff Maggert, and he is the one who has put the most distance between Tiger Woods and Masters history.

With a 6-under-par 66 Saturday afternoon at Augusta National Golf Club, Maggert made the stunning transformation from stealth contender to third-round leader of the 67th Masters. Maggert has a 54-hole total of 5-under-par 211 for a two-stroke lead over Mike Weir, who had a 75 Saturday.

"I'm really looking forward to (today)," Maggert said. "That's the best way I can put it. I would like to play well and win and have a taste of what it feels like to win a major."

— *Steve Campbell*
Houston Chronicle

Ricky Barnes, who had fantasies of winning the Masters as an amateur, found out why they call it Amen Corner in Saturday's third round at Augusta National.

The University of Arizona senior was cruising along at 2 under, 4 shots out of the lead through 10 holes, but bogeyed the 11th hole and double-bogeyed the 12th. After a birdie at 13, he also bogeyed the 17th and 18th.

It added up to a back nine of 40 and left the reigning U.S. Amateur champion at 2-over 218, 7 shots out of the lead.

Hunter Mahan whom Barnes beat in the Amateur final, also was at 2 over.

"The bogeys on the last two holes really leaves a sour taste in your mouth," Barnes said. "I hung in there until that."

— *John Davis*
The Arizona Republic

THE LEADERS' CARDS

PAR	4	5	4	3	4	3	4	5	4	36	4	4	3	5	4	5	3	4	4	36	72	TOTAL
J. MAGGERT	4	5	4	3	4	2	3	5	4	34	3	6	3	4	3	5	2	3	3	32	66	211
M. WEIR	4	4	4	3	5	3	3	5	5	36	4	5	3	6	4	4	4	5	4	39	75	213
V. SINGH	4	4	4	3	4	3	4	5	4	35	4	5	2	5	4	4	2	4	5	35	70	214
D. TOMS	5	5	3	3	5	4	3	5	4	37	4	5	3	4	3	4	3	3	4	33	70	214
P. MICKELSON	5	4	4	4	4	4	3	4	5	37	4	4	3	4	4	5	3	4	4	35	72	215
J. OLAZABAL	5	5	4	3	4	3	3	5	4	36	5	4	3	5	3	5	2	4	4	35	71	215
T. WOODS	4	4	4	3	4	2	3	5	4	33	4	3	3	4	4	4	3	4	4	33	66	215

◯ Eagle ◯ Birdie ☐ Bogey ☐ Dbl Bogey or higher

2003 MASTERS • AUGUSTA NATIONAL GOLF CLUB

54-HOLE LEADERS

J. Maggert	211
M. Weir	213
D. Toms	214
V. Singh	214
P. Mickelson	215
J. Olazabal	215
T. Woods	215
J. Byrd	216
J. Furyk	216
L. Mattiace	216

THIRD ROUND SCORING

ROUNDS	49
BELOW 70	4
BELOW PAR	17
PAR	6
OVER PAR	26
80+	1
SCORING AVG.	73.285
LOW SCORE	J. Maggert, T. Woods, 66
HIGH SCORE	J. Rollins, 80

STAT LEADERS

DRIVING DISTANCE
D. Love III, 303 yards

DRIVING ACCURACY
N. Faldo, 14 of 14 fairways

GREENS IN REGULATION
T. Woods, 15 of 18

TOTAL PUTTS
M. O'Meara, 19

(Opposite page): Jeff Maggert, left, and David Toms exchanged traditional handshakes at the end of the third round. Maggert captured the 54-hole lead with a 6-under-par 66. (Left): With a picture-perfect blue sky above, Phil Mickelson pitches onto the green in a round that left him four shots off the 54-hole lead.

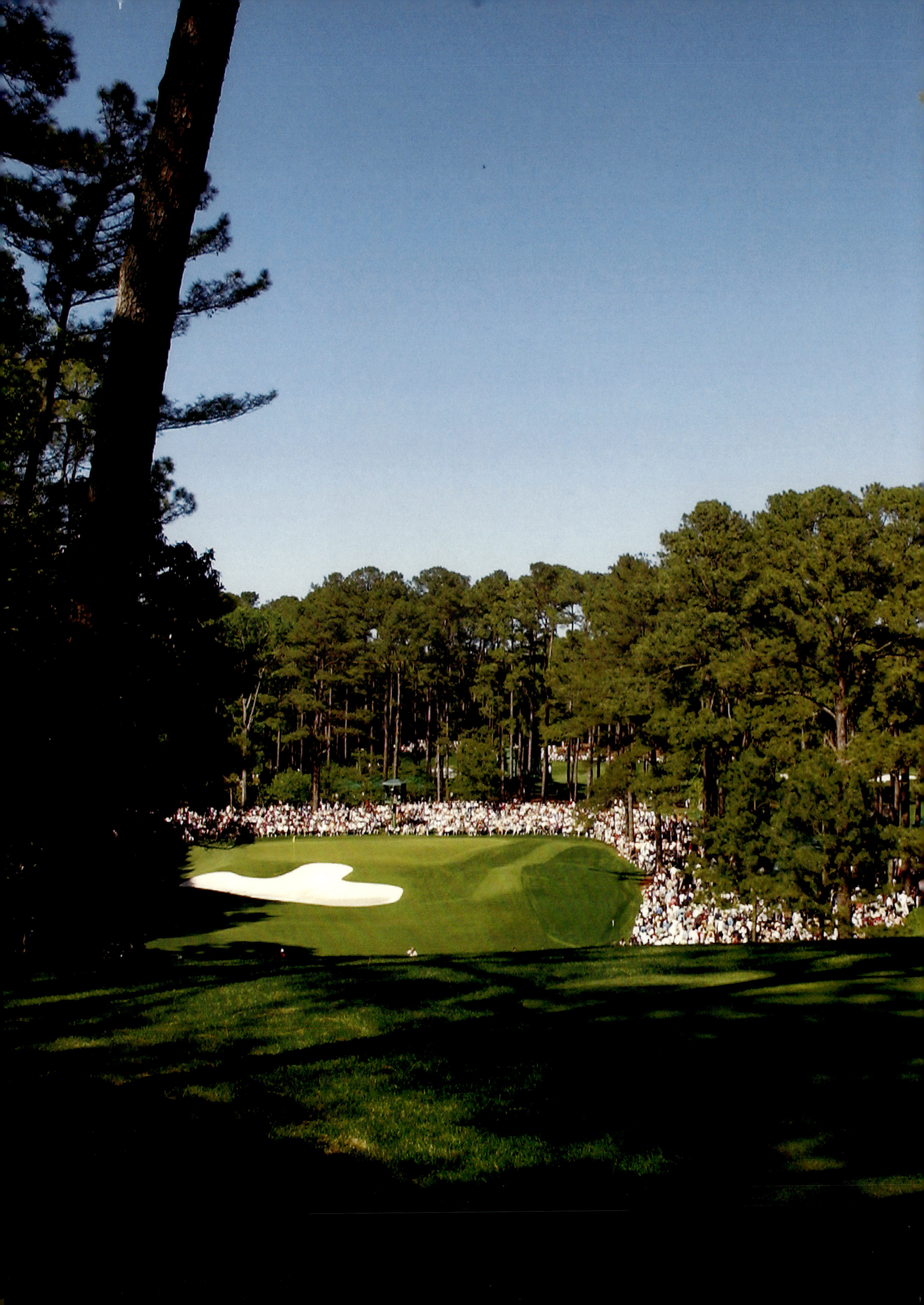

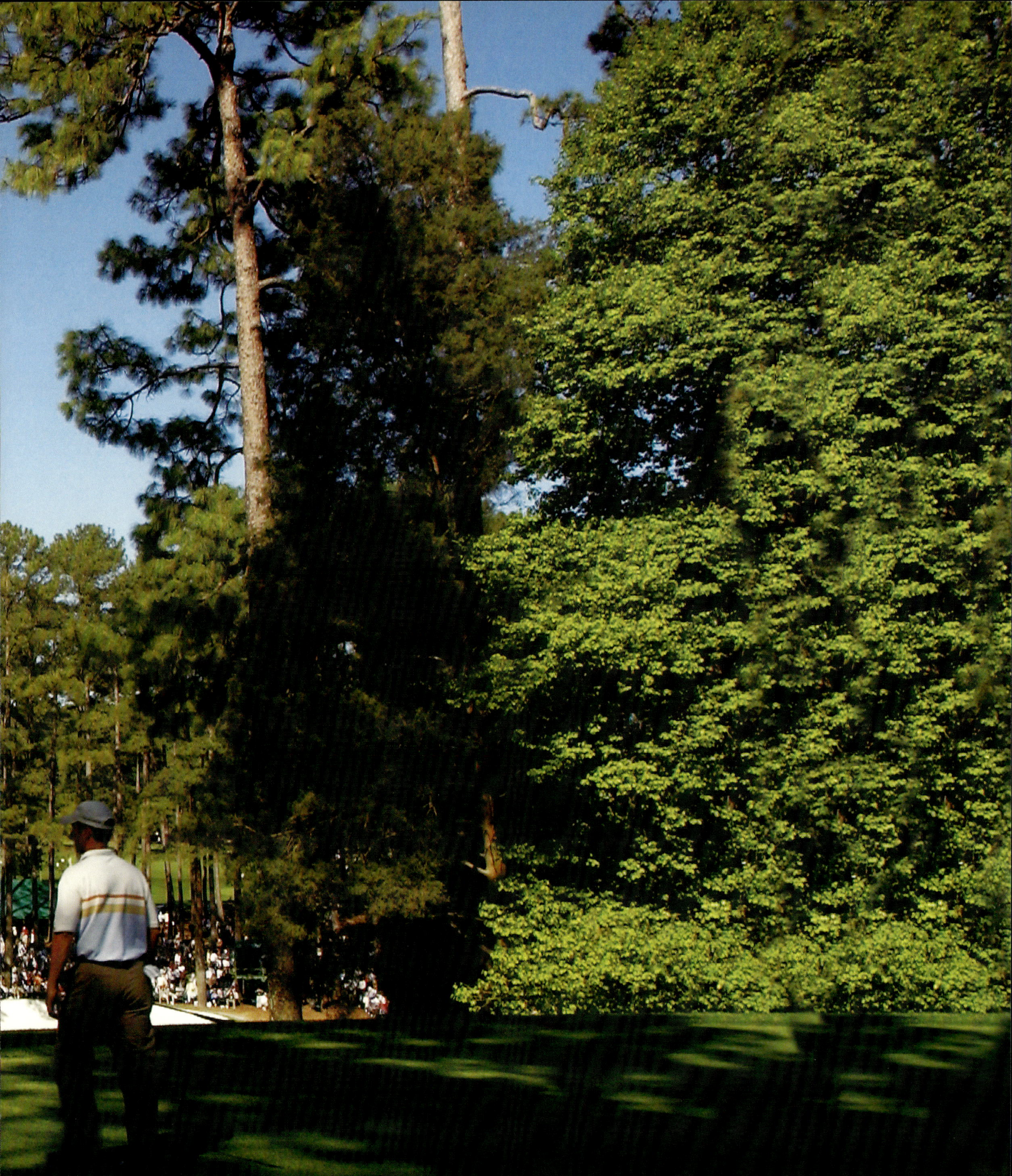

ROUND FOUR 2003

It's No Left-handed Compliment; Weir's Stellar Play Wins Masters

Every time Mike Weir needed to make a crucial putt in the final round he did en route to victory.

At his defining career moment, Mike Weir let his guard down.

But only slightly. He raised his arms skyward, let a big smile cross his face, and felt the good-all-over glow any Masters champion feels at the moment of elation.

When Weir defeated Len Mattiace with a bogey on the first extra playoff hole, it marked his first major championship of his six-year PGA Tour career.

"It was an incredible day," said the 32-year-old of his final round 68 and 7-under-par total of 281.

"I couldn't ask to play much better and it was nice to go bogey-free on Sunday in the final round of the Masters."

Weir won his playoff against Len Mattiace, who shot a final round 65. It was the first playoff since 1990 when Nick Faldo defeated Ray Floyd in a two-hole playoff.

Weir became the first left-handed golfer to win a major championship since New Zealander Bob Charles won the 1963 British Open.

The two players finished two strokes ahead of Phil Mickelson (68 - 283), three ahead of Jim Furyk (68 - 284), and five ahead of third round leader Jeff Maggert (75 - 286) who faltered with a seven on a par 4 and an eight on a par 3.

Seven of the 49 players finished under par for the 72 holes.

Three-time champion Tiger Woods, who attempted to win an unprecedented third straight Masters, suffered through a double-bogey six on the par-4 third hole en route to a final round 75 and 290 total. Woods finished tied for 15th.

"It was one of those weeks where I couldn't get anything going," said Woods. "I was in and out."

The near-miss by Mattiace in his first professional appearance at the Masters almost wrote a storybook ending.

Weir's victory came when he hit the par-4 10th hole in two and three-putted from 30 feet.

Mattiace had made Weir's winning putt elementary,

Mike Weir kept one eye on his golf game and the other on the Masters scoreboard early in the final round.

however. He had pulled his second shot left of the green and was stymied by a tree. He was forced to play away from the hole and then ran his first putt, one of great speed, from 30 feet to the back fringe of the green. He missed coming back.

The 12th playoff in Tournament history, ended a day of peaks and valleys for those at the top of the leader board.

Sunshine came to Augusta National Golf Club for a second straight day.

Balmy temperatures and light winds faced those chasing the prestigious title.

But it was evident from the start that first Weir and then Mattiace had a Green Jacket in their sights.

Out five groups from the end of the field, Mattiace shot out of the gate with a fury previously unseen.

He was playing in his first Masters as a professional - he played as a U.S. Walker Cup amateur selection in 1988 - and slowly crept up the leader board.

Mattiace, a 35-year-old from Jacksonville, Fla., and a two-time winner on the PGA Tour, began the day at even par, made four birdies in his first 10 holes causing everyone to sit up and take notice.

"Starting five shots back I knew I needed some help from the (other) guys," he said. "But if they were not on their game, I'd like to be able to make a move.

"My goal was to make six birdies and I beat my goals today."

Mattiace made his big move, however, at the 510-yard, par-5 13th hitting a 4-wood off a right-to-left hanging lie onto the green 10 feet away and sinking the putt for an eagle three.

"It was a great shot, one yard from going in the creek though," said Mattiace.

Mattiace stretched that one-stroke lead to two two holes later with another birdie. Weir kept pace, however.

In the end the 2003 Masters champion birdied the par-5 15th and heard the gallery's reaction as Mattiace bogeyed the 72nd hole, hitting his tee shot in the pine straw on the right, pitching back onto the fairway, and then hitting a 9-iron 35 feet beyond the hole location. He two-putted for his only bogey of the day.

Weir, now tied with Mattiace with a hole to play, hit his 4-iron 45 feet short and on the lower slope of the green.

He putted tentatively and left it six or seven feet short.

But as he had done all week, he sank the putt to force a playoff. He then took care of business, albeit in an unusual way with a winning bogey.

Weir, in only his fourth Masters, knew a playoff lie ahead; so did Mattiace.

He felt the energy flow, though.

"I was fatigued last night," said Weir who suffered from third round leg cramps but slept 10 hours and awoke refreshed for the final round.

"My legs felt more stable over the ball today."

Weir hit 12 of 18 greens and 11 of 14 fairways in the final round. He needed only 26 putts to secure his first Masters title.

Mattiace's near miss left him emotionally spent afterward, but, he said, as time goes by his performance will make him even prouder.

"I knew one would win the playoff and one would lose it," he said of a final round which saw him hit 13 of 18 greens in regulation and saw him take only 24 putts.

"I gave it my all. I didn't get out of focus all day. I was looking (at my target) and hitting it. It was my best major championship finish ever."

That left Weir alone to bask in the glow of three wins only 15 weeks into 2003.

The elation was, well, heady.

"It was a gut-wrenching day and I wouldn't wish that last putt (on No. 18) on anybody," Weir said.

"I don't own a green jacket. I was hoping some day this would be my first one. And I'm glad to be wearing it right now, believe me."

Weir found himself tied for the lead in the 1999 PGA Championship at Medinah. In the final pairing with Tiger Woods, Weir shot 80 and finished T10, eight strokes back of Woods' winning total.

It wasn't a lesson lost on the 5-foot-9, 155-pound golfer.

"There's been a lot of hard work since that PGA Championship," he said. "I worked on making my game more consistent, making my putting more consistent."

Weir will tell you he's won five times since rededicating himself with a stronger work ethic.

But none of the wins, the left-handed golfer said, were more meaningful than his first Masters.

"It took me six years to get on tour," said the man who spent his early career playing the Canadian Tour and Australasia Tour to gain experience and confidence.

"And it's an unbelievable progression that I've finally gotten here, but I think even back then I believed that I would get here somehow."

Over four days in April, on a world-famous and difficult golf course, Weir finally found out he'd arrived.

My how he'd arrived.

(Opposite page): Tiger Woods pondered the task at hand during the final round. (Left): Len Mattiace waves to the Masters patrons following a scintillating 7-under-par 65 that pulled him into a playoff with Mike Weir.

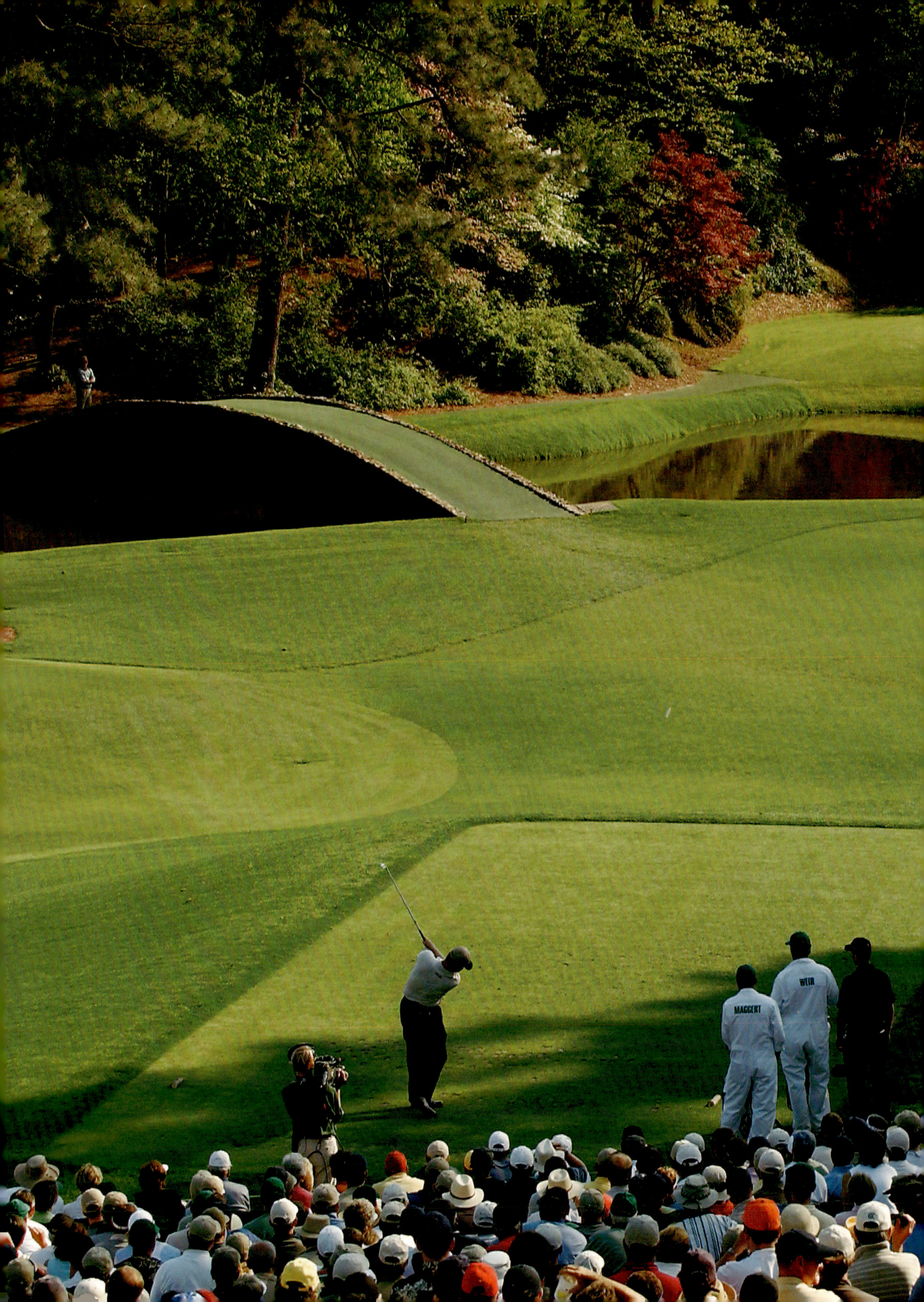
MAGGERT
WEIR

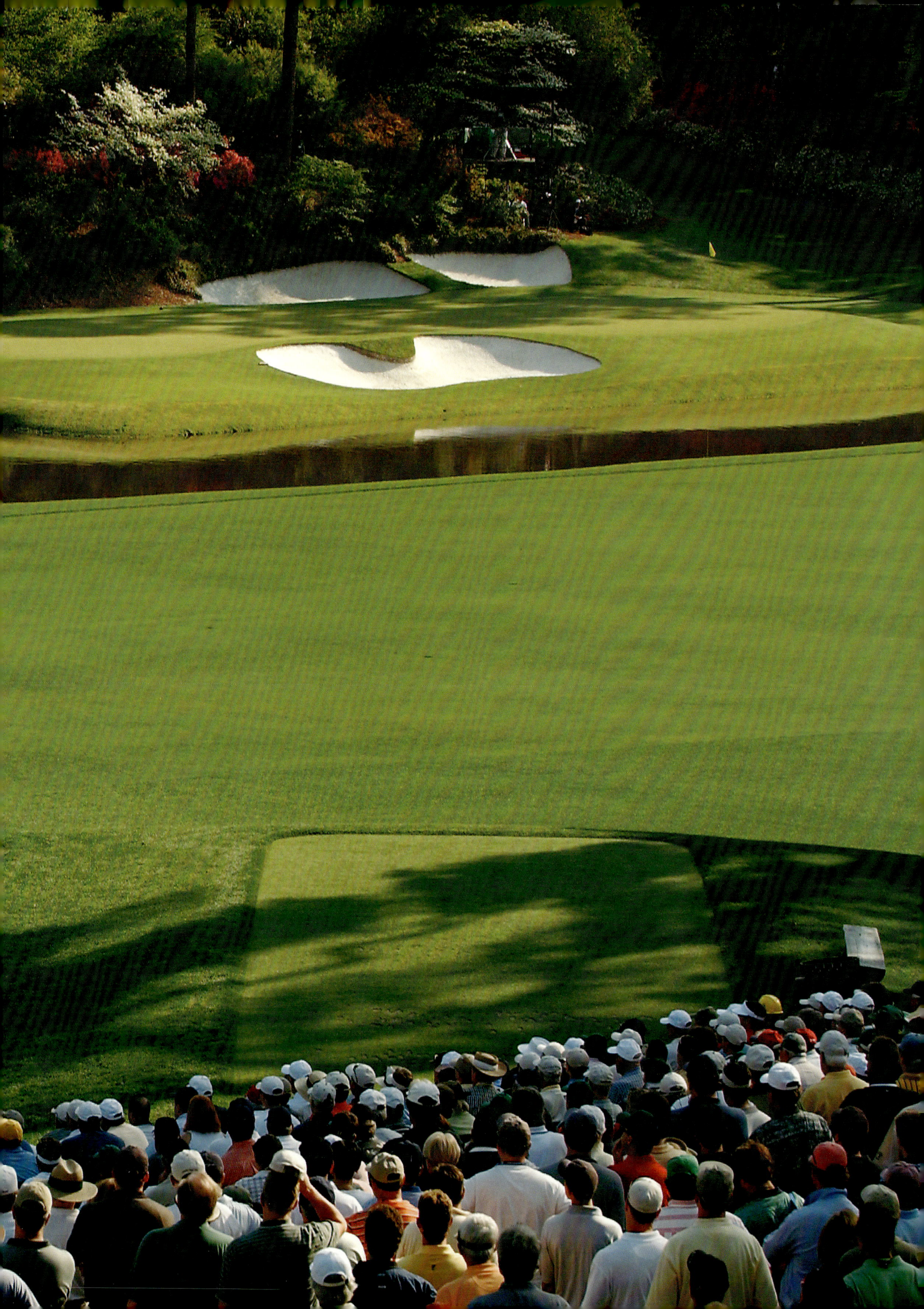

(Above): Jeff Maggert ran into trouble in the final round when his second shot from a fairway bunker at the third hole struck him for a two-stroke penalty. Maggert made a triple bogey on the hole. (Opposite page): Third-round leader Jeff Maggert, left, congratulated a playoff-bound Mike Weir following their final round pairing.

Maggert Faced A Difficult Day

The third round leader couldn't overcome two disastrous holes.

Some days golf can be a very cruel game.

Jeff Maggert found that out during the final round of the Masters.

As the 54-hole leader at 5-under-par 211, Maggert began the day with a two stroke lead on the field. It quickly evaporated and Maggert's dream of his first major championship would have to wait another day.

In the end Maggert shot 75 and finished solo fifth at 286.

In some ways it was a testimony to his character but, oh, what a painful way to find out what you're made of.

"I'd like to play a couple of holes again," said the 39-year-old Texan. "It was a very strange day. There were a couple of miscues. Funny things happen sometimes."

Two holes - the 350-yard, par-4 third and the 155-yard, par-3 12th - ended his championship hopes.

At the third Maggert's tee shot, a 2-iron played for position, found the edge of the left fairway bunker. He tried to play a 53-degree sand wedge back to the fairway but hit it thin.

That shot came off the bunker lip and ricocheted off his chest for a two-stroke penalty under the Rules of Golf© (19-2b). He played his fifth shot onto the fringe of the green, chipped 15 feet beyond the hole location and one-putted for a triple-bogey seven.

"I didn't want that incident to be the mark of my day," said Maggert.

It dropped Maggert from five under par to two under par and handed eventual champion Mike Weir the lead at the time.

Maggert birdied the par-4 fifth hole and the par-4 10th hole and seemed to have steadied his course once more.

Then disaster struck again at the difficult 12th.

He pulled a 7-iron into the back bunker and it settled into the slope.

"A bad break," said the Houstonian. "It was a lousy lie. I needed to blast (the shot) at the edge of the fringe."

Instead the club caught the ball flush and scuttled over the green into Rae's Creek.

He dropped under penalty on the opposite side of the creek closer to the tee and then hit his fourth shot heavy into the water again. After another penalty stroke, Maggert's sixth shot found the green and he two-putted from about eight feet for an eight. It moved him to one over par and he was never a factor again.

Maggert did rebound with birdies at Nos. 14-16 but his pain was felt by Weir.

"It was difficult to watch," said Weir of Maggert's two holes that cost him a chance at the win.

"But Jeff conducted himself very well out there under difficult circumstances. Things like that seem to happen sometimes. It's just the phenomenon of Augusta National."

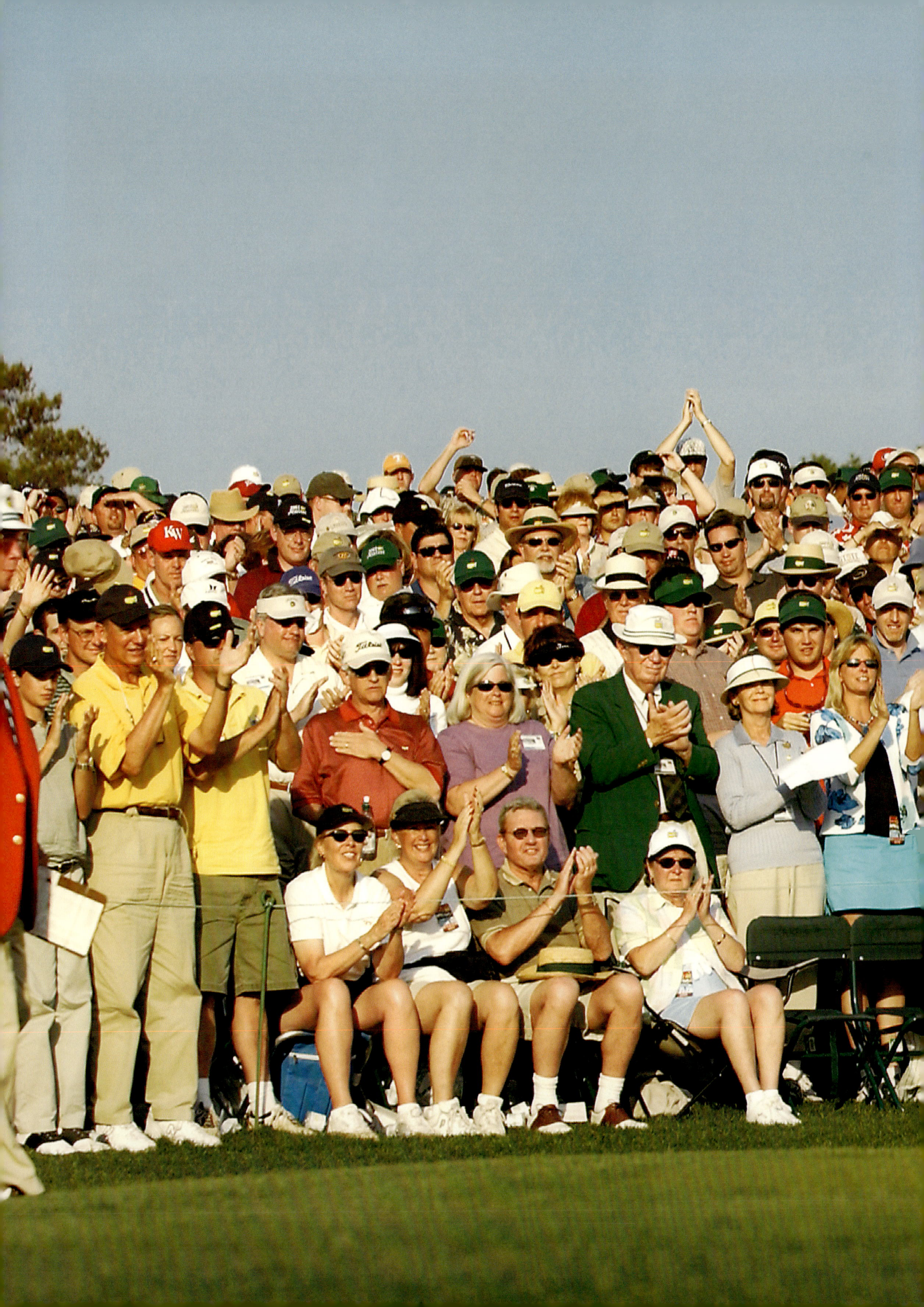
KW

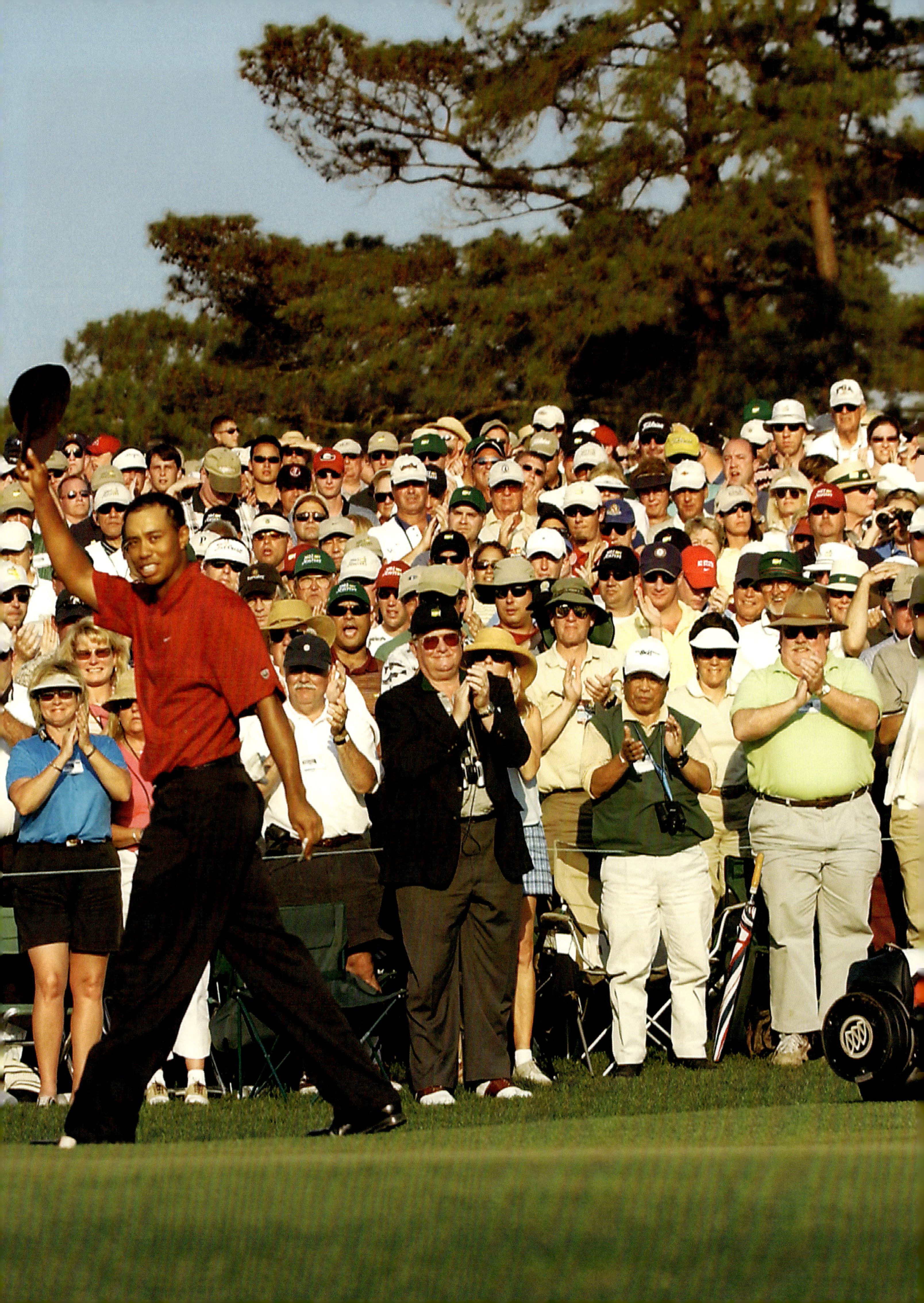

Did You Know?

- Until Mike Weir's victory at the 2003 Masters Tournament, the best finish by a Canadian was a second place finish by George Knudson in 1969.

- No player in this year's Masters had four rounds at par or better. The last time that happened was in 1983.

- The last time someone made eight or higher on No. 12 was in 1994 by Nick Price and Mike Standly. Jeff Maggert made an eight at No. 12 in the final round this year.

- Mike Weir's bogey-free final round (in regulation) makes him only the fourth Masters champion to finish without a bogey. The others are Jimmy Demaret (1940), Ben Hogan (1951) and Doug Ford (1957).

- Until he made a bogey at the 18th hole in the final round, Len Mattiace was on course to tie the low final round scoring record of 64. That mark is shared by Maurice Bembridge (1974), Hale Irwin (1975), Gary Player (1978), Greg Norman (1988) and David Toms (1998). Of the five golfers, only Player went on to win the Masters that year.

What They're Writing

He's not the biggest guy out there, but his heart is as big as anyone's and he now moves right up there alongside all the great Canadian sporting heroes with a performance that we in our country will be talking about for a long time.

As in forever. In terms of individual sports, Mike Weir's (Masters) victory in a men's professional major championship ranks right up there, in the Canadian pantheon, with, say, Donovan Bailey's 1996 Olympic gold medal in the 100 meters.

Maybe with Lennox Lewis as heavyweight champion of the world, but let's not get into that flag flap again. This was a moment for all Canadians to take pride in.

Weir's that kind of guy, too, a little tightly wound at times, but decent, extremely likeable and possessing a strong sense of right and wrong.

- Dave Perkins
Toronto Star

Out on the prettiest course in the world, Mike Weir was moving through the back nine, resolute.

He was following the prescription that the late George Knudson once gave for success in golf: Get the job done, any way. Stay strong. Make it happen.

So it was that Weir got mentally stronger as the day wore on, and as he worked his way toward becoming the first Canadian to win a men's professional major championship.

What a study in discipline.

- Lorne Rubenstein
Toronto Globe & Mail

What They're Writing
(continued)

Some view it as one of his endearing characteristics. Others consider it his fatal flaw.

To Phil Mickelson, the cup is always half full. Even in the wake of what might appear to be wrenching defeats, Mickelson prefers to accentuate the positive.

He did it again Sunday after coming up painfully short in his latest quest to win the Masters Tournament.

"You can't look at success in wins and losses," said Mickelson, who finished third at the Masters for the third-straight year. "You have to look at success on your own terms."

- Larry Williams
The Augusta Chronicle

With the sun setting over Augusta National, Tiger Woods gave it away. That would be the green jacket he helped lift over the shoulders of a new Masters champion. That would be Mike Weir. Not Tiger.

The weather was bad early in this major and, Woods would say, he wasn't much better, shooting that crushing 76 in the rain-soaked first round to dig his cleats deep in the Georgia mud.

Three rounds later, Woods' biggest prime-time appearance this Masters Sunday showed him slapping Weir on the shoulders, telling Weir, "Congratulations, buddy," without giving off a whiff of petulance or regret.

- Laura Vecsey
The Baltimore Sun

The first thing anybody thought when Len Mattiace started crying is that the loss got to him. That's how we think most of the time. His eyes flared red, and his voice choked, and all around him were people shaking their heads.

Poor guy lost in a playoff at the Masters. He was so close. Can't blame a man for crying.

Thing is, it was a different kind of crying, the kind you don't see much from people who lose.

Len Mattiace was just so doggone proud.

- Joe Posnanski
Kansas City Star

(Opposite page): Len Mattiace enjoyed his best finish ever in a major. (Above): Korea's K.J. Choi exhorted this putt to find the bottom of the cup during the Masters.

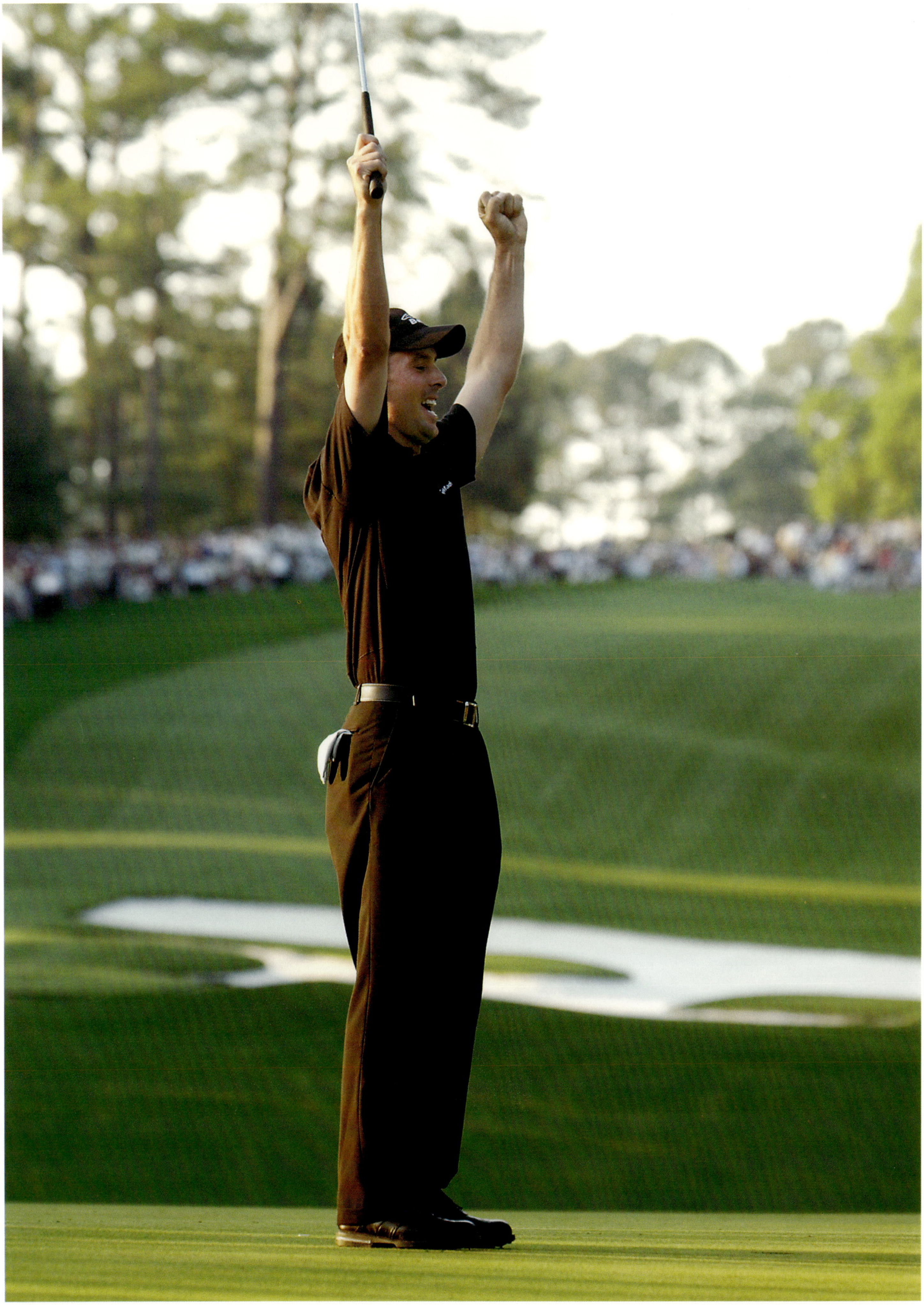

(Opposite page): Mike Weir raised his hands in jubilation after sinking his winning putt and claimed his first Masters title.
(Above): Floridian Len Mattiace celebrated one of six birdies in the final round when he sank this putt at the 16th hole. Mattiace shot 65 but lost in a playoff to Mike Weir.

THE LEADERS' CARDS

PAR	4	5	4	3	4	3	4	5	4	36	4	4	3	5	4	5	3	4	4	36	72	TOTAL
M. WEIR	4	(4)	4	3	4	(2)	4	5	4	34	4	4	3	(4)	4	(4)	3	4	4	34	68	281
L. MATTIACE	4	(4)	(3)	3	4	3	4	(4)	4	33	(3)	4	3	(3)	4	(4)	(2)	4	[5]	32	65	281
P. MICKELSON	4	(4)	4	3	4	[4]	(3)	5	4	35	4	4	3	(4)	4	(4)	3	4	(3)	33	68	283
J. FURYK	4	(4)	4	3	4	3	4	(4)	4	34	4	4	[4]	5	4	(3)	3	(3)	4	34	68	284
J. MAGGERT	4	5	[7]	3	(3)	3	4	5	4	38	(3)	4	[8]	5	(3)	(4)	(2)	4	4	37	75	286
E. ELS	(3)	5	[5]	3	[5]	(2)	4	(4)	(3)	34	4	[5]	3	(4)	4	5	3	4	4	36	70	287
V. SINGH	4	(4)	4	3	[5]	3	4	5	4	36	(3)	(3)	[4]	[6]	4	[6]	3	4	4	37	73	287

PLAYOFF - SUDDEN DEATH

PAR	4	5	4	3	4	3	4	5	4	36	4	4	3	5	4	5	3	4	4	36	72	
M. WEIR	[5]									5												
L. MATTIACE	[6]									6												

◯ Eagle ○ Birdie ▢ Bogey ▢ Dbl Bogey or higher

STAT LEADERS

DRIVING DISTANCE   H. Mahan, 314 yards
DRIVING ACCURACY   L. Roberts, J. Sluman 13 of 14 fairways
GREENS IN REGULATION   R. Allenby, P. Mickelson, R. Goosen, J. Sluman, 14 of 18
TOTAL PUTTS   D. Love III, 22

FOURTH ROUND SCORING

ROUNDS	49	**80+**	0
BELOW 70	5	**SCORING AVG.**	73.083
BELOW PAR	15	**LOW SCORE**	L. Mattiace, 65
PAR	2	**HIGH SCORE**	R. Moore,
OVER PAR	32		J. Kelly, 79

2003 MASTERS • AUGUSTA NATIONAL GOLF CLUB

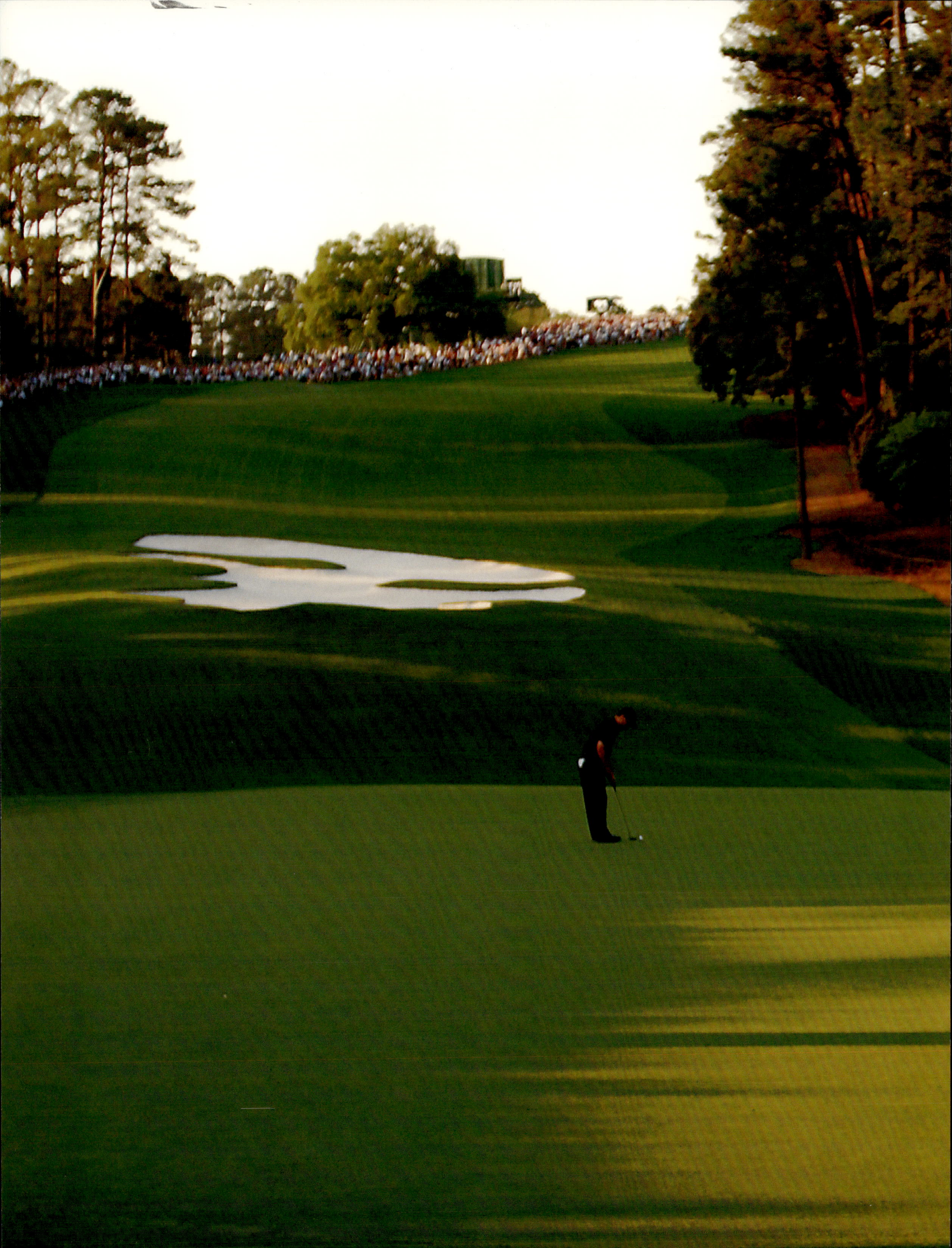

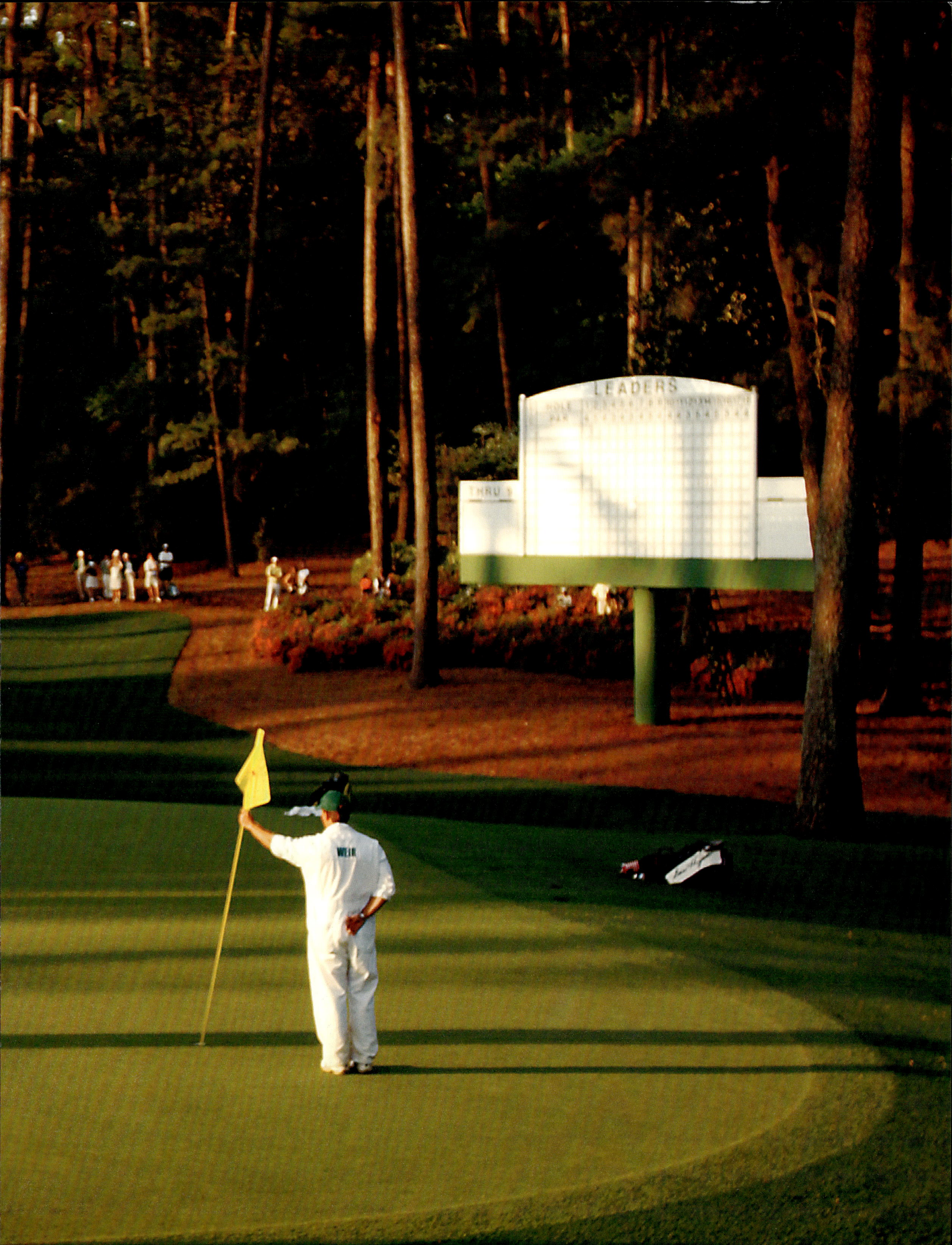
LEADERS
THRU

Three-time Masters champion Tiger Woods, left, helps the 2003 champion, Mike Weir, on with his coveted 42 regular Green Jacket at the awards ceremony.

CHAMPION 2003

Oh, Canada!

Mike Weir becomes the first Canadian and the first left-handed golfer to ever win the Masters Tournament.

When he was a child growing up, Mike Weir knew hockey was king in Canada. It was his country's national past-time after all. But Weir knew he was probably too small for professional hockey - he's just 5-foot-9, 155 pounds now at age 32 - and the challenge of golf called him longingly.

The metamorphosis from hockey player to 2003 Masters Tournament winner came innocently enough. Weir attended the Canadian Open at 10 and became fascinated with the game.

And he didn't let the fact he was left-handed bother him. Or the fact that Canadian golfers' success was limited to the likes of George Knudson, Stan Leonard, Al Balding and Moe Norman.

Weir wrote Masters champion Jack Nicklaus, asking the Golden Bear if he should switch to a right-handed golfer.

Nicklaus' return letter provided both the encouragement Weir needed and the impetus he wanted to abandon hockey and baseball.

"I did write to him at 13," said Weir of his letter to Nicklaus, "and I still have the letter in my office. He said to stick with my natural swing."

Weir did. His father, Rich, now a retired chemical engineer, set up a driving net in the garage at their Brights Grove home outside Sarnia.

Practically every winter day the youngster could be found hitting balls in the unheated garage.

Michael Richard Weir, born May 12, 1970, had the golf bug and nothing was going to stop him from success.

At age 16 he won the Canadian Juvenile Championship and later added the Canadian Ontario Amateur Championship to his resume.

After attending Brigham Young University in Utah, he turned pro in 1992 and joined the Canadian Tour in 1993 and although he struggled from 1994-96, Weir broke through in 1997, winning that Tour's Order of Merit as the leading player.

Maybe he was on his way to the PGA Tour.

But five unsuccessful attempts at PGA Tour Qualifying School before 1998 provided a harsh lesson in reality.

He played in Australia and in Canada to gain experience and confidence. He worked hard. Oh, did he work hard.

"It took me five years of going to qualifying school to get out here," Weir said after his 2003 Masters triumph, his sixth on the PGA Tour.

"I can remember many times that I was missing cut after cut on the Australian Tour and I was by myself and didn't have any money. You're out on the (practice) range by yourself practicing until

(Above): 2003 Masters Tournament winner Mike Weir and three-time champion Tiger Woods shared a special moment at the awards ceremony. (Opposite page): Newly crowned champion Mike Weir, resplendent in his new Green Jacket, waved to the appreciative patrons attending the ceremony.

you can't see in front of you. I'll always have those things in my memory bank, those tough times. If anything contributes to my determination it is because I know how hard it is to get here."

Weir said his success at the 2003 Masters is like life.

"The message is perseverance," he said. "not just in golf, but in anything in which you want to succeed. Be dedicated, work hard, treat people with integrity and good things will happen."

Those around him at BYU knew Weir was something special.

"How tough can you be?" then assistant BYU coach Bruce Brockbank said of Weir's character, which shone brightly at Augusta National Golf Club. "It just oozes out of his veins, the guts the kid has. There have been a lot of people come through the program who were more talented, but there was something about him."

With his first major championship, Weir has become a major symbol to Canadian golfers.

It is a role he relishes.

"I'm trying to do what I can do and hopefully some of the younger kids in Canada will take a passion for the game," said Weir.

"I hope the programs and the development of golf in Canada is getting better. Hopefully I have a little influence on that."

But, said the new champion, don't forget the most important lesson, one he, himself, has learned the hard way.

"My message as a role model is the same as it was before - the way I got here," he said of the hard work and determination it took to become a Masters winner.

Remember that, said Weir, and you'll succeed in anything in life.

MIKE WEIR
2003 MASTERS CHAMPION

BIRTH DATE: May 12, 1970
HOME: Draper, Utah
BIRTHPLACE: Sarnia, Ontario, Canada
AGE: 32 **HT:** 5'9" **WT:** 155
TURNED PRO: 1992
JOINED PGA TOUR: 1998
PGA TOUR VICTORIES:
2003 Bob Hope Chrysler Classic, Nissan Open; 2001 The Tour Championship; 2000 WGC-American Express Championship; 1999 Air Canada Championship
OTHER VICTORIES:
1997 BC TEL Pacific Open (Canada), Canadian Masters

MASTERS RECORD

YEAR	FINISH	SCORE
2000	T28	293
2001	T27	287
2002	T24	290
2003	WON	281

2003 MASTERS • AUGUSTA NATIONAL GOLF CLUB

2003 MASTERS • AUGUSTA NATIONAL GOLF CLUB

MASTERS CHAMPIONS

2003	Mike Weir	281
2002	Tiger Woods	276
2001	Tiger Woods	272
2000	Vijay Singh	278
1999	Jose Maria Olazabal	280
1998	Mark O'Meara	279
1997	Tiger Woods	270
1996	Nick Faldo	276
1995	Ben Crenshaw	274
1994	Jose Maria Olazabal	279
1993	Bernhard Langer	277
1992	Fred Couples	275
1991	Ian Woosnam	277
1990	Nick Faldo	278
1989	Nick Faldo	283
1988	Sandy Lyle	281
1987	Larry Mize	285
1986	Jack Nicklaus	279
1985	Bernhard Langer	282
1984	Ben Crenshaw	277
1983	Seve Ballesteros	280
1982	Craig Stadler	284
1981	Tom Watson	280
1980	Seve Ballesteros	275
1979	Fuzzy Zoeller	280
1978	Gary Player	277
1977	Tom Watson	276
1976	Raymond Floyd	271
1975	Jack Nicklaus	276
1974	Gary Player	278
1973	Tommy Aaron	283
1972	Jack Nicklaus	286
1971	Charles Coody	279
1970	Billy Casper	279
1969	George Archer	281
1968	Bob Goalby	277
1967	Gay Brewer	280
1966	Jack Nicklaus	288
1965	Jack Nicklaus	271
1964	Arnold Palmer	276
1963	Jack Nicklaus	286
1962	Arnold Palmer	280
1961	Gary Player	280
1960	Arnold Palmer	282
1959	Art Wall	284
1958	Arnold Palmer	284
1957	Doug Ford	283
1956	Jack Burke	289
1955	Cary Middlecoff	279
1954	Sam Snead	289
1953	Ben Hogan	274
1952	Sam Snead	286
1951	Ben Hogan	280
1950	Jimmy Demaret	283
1949	Sam Snead	282
1948	Claude Harmon	279
1947	Jimmy Demaret	281
1946	Herman Keiser	282
1942	Byron Nelson	280
1941	Craig Wood	280
1940	Jimmy Demaret	280
1939	Ralph Guldahl	279
1938	Henry Picard	285
1937	Byron Nelson	283
1936	Horton Smith	285
1935	Gene Sarazen	282
1934	Horton Smith	284

Ricky Barnes of Stockton, Calif., held the low amateur trophy high for all to see after he recorded rounds of 69-74-75-73 – 291 to finish 21st overall. Barnes was one of three amateurs to make the cut.

FINAL SCORING

ROUNDS	283
BELOW 70	15
BELOW PAR	55
PAR	25
OVER PAR	203
80+	27
SCORING AVG.	74.7
LOW SCORE	65
	L. Mattiace, Round 4
HIGH SCORE	92
	T. Aaron, Round 1

TOURNAMENT STAT LEADERS

DRIVING DISTANCE
H. Mahan, 296 yards

DRIVING ACCURACY
N. Faldo, 48 of 56

GREENS IN REGULATION
R. Beem, R. Goosen, 50 of 72

TOTAL PUTTS
M. O'Meara, J. Maggert, 101

RECAP 2003
RESULTS & STATISTICS

	PLAYER		SCORE				PRIZE MONEY
1	Mike Weir (Canada)	70	68	75	68	281	$1,080,000
	Low Professional: Gold Medal						
	Sterling Silver Replica Masters Trophy						
2	Len Mattiace	73	74	69	65	281	$648,000
	Runner-up: Silver Medal						
	Sterling Silver Salver						
	Crystal Vase, Day's Low Score (65), Round 4						
	Pair of Crystal Goblets, Eagle, Round 4, Hole 13						
3	Phil Mickelson	73	70	72	68	283	$408,000
4	Jim Furyk	73	72	71	68	284	$288,000
	Pair of Crystal Goblets, Eagle, Round 4, Hole 15						
5	Jeff Maggert	72	73	66	75	286	$240,000
	Crystal Vase, Day's Low Score (66), Round 3						
T6	Ernie Els (South Africa)	79	66	72	70	287	$208,500
	Crystal Vase, Day's Low Score (66), Round 2						
	Pair of Crystal Goblets, Eagle, Round 3, Hole 7						
T6	Vijay Singh (Fiji)	73	71	70	73	287	$208,500
T8	Jonathan Byrd	74	71	71	72	288	$162,000
T8	Mark O'Meara	76	71	70	71	288	$162,000
T8	Jose Maria Olazabal (Spain)	73	71	71	73	288	$162,000
T8	David Toms	71	73	70	74	288	$162,000
T8	Scott Verplank	76	73	70	69	288	$162,000
T13	Tim Clark (South Africa)	72	75	71	71	289	$120,000
T13	Retief Goosen (South Africa)	73	74	72	70	289	$120,000
T15	Rich Beem	74	72	71	73	290	$93,000
	Pair if Crystal Goblets, Eagle, Round 4, Hole 5						
T15	Angel Cabrera (Argentina)	76	71	71	72	290	$93,000
T15	K.J. Choi (Korea)	76	69	72	73	290	$93,000
T15	Paul Lawrie (Scotland)	72	72	73	73	290	$93,000
T15	Davis Love III	77	71	71	71	290	$93,000
T15	Tiger Woods	76	73	66	75	290	$93,000
	Crystal Vase, Day's Low Score (66), Round 3						
21	Ricky Barnes	69	74	75	73	291	Amateur
	Low Amateur: Sterling Silver Cup						
22	Bob Estes	76	71	74	71	292	$72,000
T23	Brad Faxon	73	71	79	70	293	$57,600
T23	Scott McCarron	77	71	72	73	293	$57,600
	Pair of Crystal Goblets, Eagle, Round 2, Hole 15						
T23	Nick Price (Zimbabwe)	70	75	72	76	293	$57,600
T23	Chris Riley	76	72	70	75	293	$57,600
T23	Adam Scott (Australia)	77	72	74	70	293	$57,600
T28	Darren Clarke (N. Ireland)	66	76	78	74	294	$43,500
	Crystal Vase, Day's Low Score (66), Round 1						
	Pair of Crystal Goblets, Eagle, Round 1, Hole 15						
	Pair of Crystal Goblets, Eagle, Round 3, Hole 15						
T28	Fred Couples	73	75	69	77	294	$43,500
T28	Sergio Garcia (Spain)	69	78	74	73	294	$43,500
T28	Charles Howell III	73	72	76	73	294	$43,500
T28	Hunter Mahan	73	72	73	76	294	Amateur
	Low Amateur Runner-up: Silver Medal						
T33	Nick Faldo (England)	74	73	75	73	295	$36,375
	Pair of Crystal Goblets, Eagle, Round 2 Hole 2						
T33	Rocco Mediate	73	74	73	75	295	$36,375
T33	Loren Roberts	74	72	76	73	295	$36,375
T33	Kevin Sutherland	77	72	76	70	295	$36,375
T37	Shingo Katayama (Japan)	74	72	76	74	296	$31,650
T37	Billy Mayfair	75	70	77	74	296	$31,650
T39	Robert Allenby (Australia)	76	73	74	74	297	$27,000
T39	Craig Parry (Australia)	74	73	75	75	297	$27,000
T39	Kenny Perry	76	72	78	71	297	$27,000
T39	Justin Rose (England)	73	76	71	77	297	$27,000
T39	Phil Tataurangi (New Zealand)	75	70	74	78	297	$27,000

	PLAYER		SCORE				PRIZE MONEY
44	Jeff Sluman	75	72	76	75	298	$23,400
T45	Ryan Moore	73	74	75	79	301	Amateur
	Pair of Crystal Goblets, Eagle, Round 1, Hole 13						
T45	Pat Perez	74	73	79	75	301	$22,200
47	John Rollins	74	71	80	77	302	$21,000
48	Jerry Kelly	72	76	77	79	304	$19,800
	Pair of Crystal Goblets, Eagle, Round 1, Hole 15						
49	Craig Stadler	76	73	79	77	305	$18,600

THE FOLLOWING PLAYERS DID NOT MAKE THE CUT AT 149

PLAYER						
Padraig Harrington (Ireland)	77	73			150	$5,000
Scott Hoch	77	73			150	$5,000
Shigeki Maruyama (Japan)	75	75			150	$5,000
Pair of Crystal Goblets, Eagle, Round 1, Hole 8						
Eduardo Romero (Argentina)	74	76			150	$5,000
Toru Taniguchi (Japan)	71	79			150	$5,000
Steve Elkington (Australia)	75	76			151	$5,000
Lee Janzen	78	73			151	$5,000
Tom Lehman	75	76			151	$5,000
Larry Mize	78	74			152	$5,000
Tom Watson	75	77			152	$5,000
Stuart Appleby (Australia)	77	76			153	$5,000
Miguel Angel Jimenez (Spain)	76	77			153	$5,000
Chad Campbell	77	77			154	$5,000
Niclas Fasth (Sweden)	81	73			154	$5,000
Toshi Izawa (Japan)	78	76			154	$5,000
Pair of Crystal Goblets, Eagle, Round 2, Hole 13						
Steve Lowery	78	76			154	$5,000
Colin Montgomerie (Scotland)	78	76			154	$5,000
Kirk Triplett	82	72			154	$5,000
Ian Woosnam (Wales)	80	74			154	$5,000
Michael Campbell (New Zealand)	78	77			155	$5,000
Ben Crenshaw	79	76			155	$5,000
Fred Funk	79	76			155	$5,000
Jay Haas	79	76			155	$5,000
Bernhard Langer (Germany)	79	76			155	$5,000
Justin Leonard	82	73			155	$5,000
Sandy Lyle (Scotland)	82	73			155	$5,000
Craig Perks (New Zealand)	80	75			155	$5,000
Fuzzy Zoeller	77	78			155	$5,000
John Cook	78	78			156	$5,000
John Huston	73	83			156	$5,000
Pair of Crystal Goblets, Eagle, Round 2, Hole 8						
Thomas Levet (France)	79	77			156	$5,000
Tom Byrum	82	75			157	$5,000
Raymond Floyd	77	80			157	$5,000
Peter Lonard (Australia)	78	82			160	$5,000
Seve Ballesteros (Spain)	77	85			162	$5,000
David Duval	79	83			162	$5,000
Jack Nicklaus	85	77			162	$5,000
Gary Player (South Africa)	82	80			162	$5,000
Alejandro Larrazabal (Spain)	82	81			163	Amateur
Charles Coody	83	81			164	$5,000
Arnold Palmer	83	83			166	$5,000
George Zahringer	82	85			167	Amateur
Tommy Aaron	92	80			172	$5,000
Chris DiMarco	82	WD			82	$5,000

Masters champions present that did not participate were George Archer, Billy Casper, Doug Ford, Bob Goalby and Byron Nelson.

2003 MASTERS • AUGUSTA NATIONAL GOLF CLUB

Chairman Hootie Johnson presided over the Masters awards ceremony on the practice green following completion of play, and he had plenty of illustrious company. 2003 Masters champion Mike Weir and three-time winner Tiger Woods, far left, were all smiles while Masters Chairman Emeritus Jack Stephens and low amateur Ricky Barnes, far right, looked on.

FINAL COURSE STATISTICS

HOLE	YARDS	PAR	AVG.	RANK	EAGLES	BIRDIES	PARS	BOGEYS	DBL BOGEYS	OTHER
1	435	4	4.296	5	0	14	179	84	7	0
2	575	5	4.859	17	1	83	165	27	6	2
3	350	4	4.046	13	0	47	184	47	5	1
4	205	3	3.222	7	0	23	181	74	6	0
5	455	4	4.229	6	1	20	184	72	6	1
6	180	3	3.222	8	0	23	184	68	9	0
7	410	4	4.035	14	1	55	167	55	6	0
8	570	5	4.940	15	2	65	175	34	6	2
9	460	4	4.211	9	0	25	182	69	8	0
OUT	3,640	36	37.060		5	355	1,601	530	59	6
10	495	4	4.313	3	0	22	166	85	8	3
11	490	4	4.412	1	0	17	152	97	17	1
12	155	3	3.303	4	0	22	182	62	13	5
13	510	5	4.915	16	3	83	145	45	5	3
14	440	4	4.197	10	0	31	173	73	7	0
15	500	5	4.771	18	5	96	150	26	6	1
16	170	3	3.141	11	0	41	172	63	6	2
17	425	4	4.130	12	0	33	191	50	10	0
18	465	4	4.410	2	0	13	158	97	13	2
IN	3,650	36	37.592		8	358	1,489	598	85	17
TOTAL	7,290	72	74.652		13	713	3,090	1,128	144	23

ALL-TIME SCORING RECORDS

LOW FIRST NINE – 30, Johnny Miller, third round, 1975; Greg Norman, fourth round, 1988.
LOW SECOND NINE – 29, Mark Calcavecchia, fourth round, 1992; David Toms, fourth round, 1998.
LOW 18 – 63, Nick Price, third round, 1986; Greg Norman, first round, 1996.
LOW FIRST ROUND – 63, Greg Norman, first round, 1996
LOW SECOND ROUND – 64, Miller Barber, 1979; Jay Haas, 1995.
LOW THIRD ROUND – 63, Nick Price, 1986.
LOW FOURTH ROUND – 64, Maurice Bembridge, 1974; Hale Irwin, 1975; Gary Player, 1978; Greg Norman, 1988; David Toms, 1998.
LOW FIRST 36 HOLES – 131, Raymond Floyd, 1976.
LOW MIDDLE 36 HOLES – 131, Tiger Woods, 1997.
LOW LAST 36 HOLES – 131, Johnny Miller, 1975.
LOW FIRST 54 HOLES – 201, Raymond Floyd, 1976; Tiger Woods, 1997.
LOW LAST 54 HOLES – 200, Tiger Woods, 1997.
LOW 72 HOLES – 270, Tiger Woods, 1997.
HIGHEST WINNING SCORE – 289, Sam Snead, 1954; Jack Burke, 1956.
LOW 18-HOLE SCORE BY FIRST-YEAR PLAYER – 64, Lloyd Mangrum, 1940; Mike Donald, 1990; David Toms, 1998.
LOW 72-HOLES BY FIRST-YEAR PLAYER – 278, Toshi Izawa, 2001.
LOW 18 BY AN AMATEUR – 66, Ken Venturi, 1956.
LOW 72 HOLES BY AN AMATEUR – 281, Charles R. Coe, 1961.

MASTERS CLUB DINNER
PAST CHAMPIONS

First Row *(left to right):* Bob Goalby, Doug Ford, Arnold Palmer, Byron Nelson, Chairman Hootie Johnson, Billy Casper, Raymond Floyd **Second Row:** Mark O'Meara, Bernhard Langer, George Archer, Tiger Woods, Seve Ballesteros, Tommy Aaron, Charles Coody, Tom Watson, Nick Faldo, Fred Couples
Third Row: Vijay Singh, Larry Mize, Jack Nicklaus, Gary Player, Jose Maria Olazabal, Sandy Lyle, Fuzzy Zoeller, Ben Crenshaw, Ian Woosnam, Craig Stadler.

AMATEUR DINNER

(Left to Right): George Zahringer, Hunter Mahan, Chairman Hootie Johnson, Alejandro Larrazabal, Ryan Moore, Ricky Barnes

COMMITTEE CHAIRMEN

(Left to Right:) Ogden M. Phipps, J. Haley Roberts Jr., George R. Wislar, William P. Payne, Edwin L. Douglass Jr., W. Lipscomb Davis Jr., Eugene M. Howerdd Jr., John H. Dobbs, John W. Harris, William W. Johnson, William T. Gary III, Joe T. Ford, H. Lawrence Parker, James E. Johnson Jr., Frank Troutman Jr., Leroy H. Simkins Jr., Hugh L. McColl Jr., John L. Murray Jr., Phil S. Harison, Charles H. Morris, H. Ray Finney

RULES COMMITTEE

(Left to Right): Bruce C. Richards, Dow Finsterwald, Ian Pattinson, James F. Vernon, Michael Reece, Mary Bea Porter-King, Emily Crisp, James E. Reinhart, Peter Burt, Paul D. Caruso Jr., Steve Carman, James T. Bunch, Cameron Jay Rains, James J. A. Halliday, David Simons, John W. Vardaman, John D. Reynolds III, Fredric C. Nelson, H. Colin Maclaine, John Whitmore, Mark Russell, M. G. Orender, Eric J. Gleacher, Ian W. L. Webb, Gordon B. B. Jeffrey, Peter Dawson, James R. Gabrielsen, Will F. Nicholson Jr., David B. Fay, Reed K. Mackenzie, Michael Bonallack, Mike Stewart, Harry W. Easterly Jr., Warren Orlick, Lew Blakey, Joe E. Black, Fred S. Ridley, Mike Shea, Andy McFee, Craig Ammerman, Ed Hoard, F. Morgan Taylor Jr., Benjamin F. Nelson, Theo Manyama, Rod Myers, Mark Wilson, Brad Gregory, Robert H. Chapman III, Stephen Ross, David Price, Charles Lanzetta, Carr McCalla, John Paramor, David Pepper, Bruce Sudderth, Stephen Cox, Eugene M. Howerdd Jr., Ron Hickman, Neil Crichton, Thomas J. Meeks, Don Essig III, Jack Connelly, Andy Yamanaka, Brian Whitcomb

GOLF WRITERS ASSOCIATION OF AMERICA

First Row *(Left to Right):* Hubert Mizell, George Willis, Hank Gola, Filip Bondy, Art Spander, George Sweda Marino Parascenzo, Kaye Kessler, Richard Mudry, Ed Sherman, Vartan Kupelian, Dave Seanor, Tom Auclair, Joe Gordon, Bud Thompson **Second Row:** James Achenbach, Brian Murphy, Bill Fields, Joel Walker, Pete Georgiady, Greg Johnson, Furman Bisher, David Mackintosh, Hiroaki Yokoyama, Barry Cronin, Reiko Takekawa, Jeff Rude, Sal Johnson, Len Shapiro, T. R. Reinman, Mark Cannizzaro, Dave Shedloski **Third Row:** Steve Elling, Mick Elliott, Joe Juliano, Neil Geoghegan, Mike Kern, Mike Dudurich, Dave Hackenberg, Lorne Rubenstein, Garry Smits, Jack Bacot, Ann Liguori, Holly Geoghegan, Scott Tolley **Fourth Row:** Larry Durland, Jack Berry, Jeff Shain, Brett Avery, Helen Ross, Dick Donovan, Terry Moore, Byron Huff, Chris Wagner, Tom Kensler, Roger Graves **Fifth Row:** Steve Campbell, Jimmy Burch

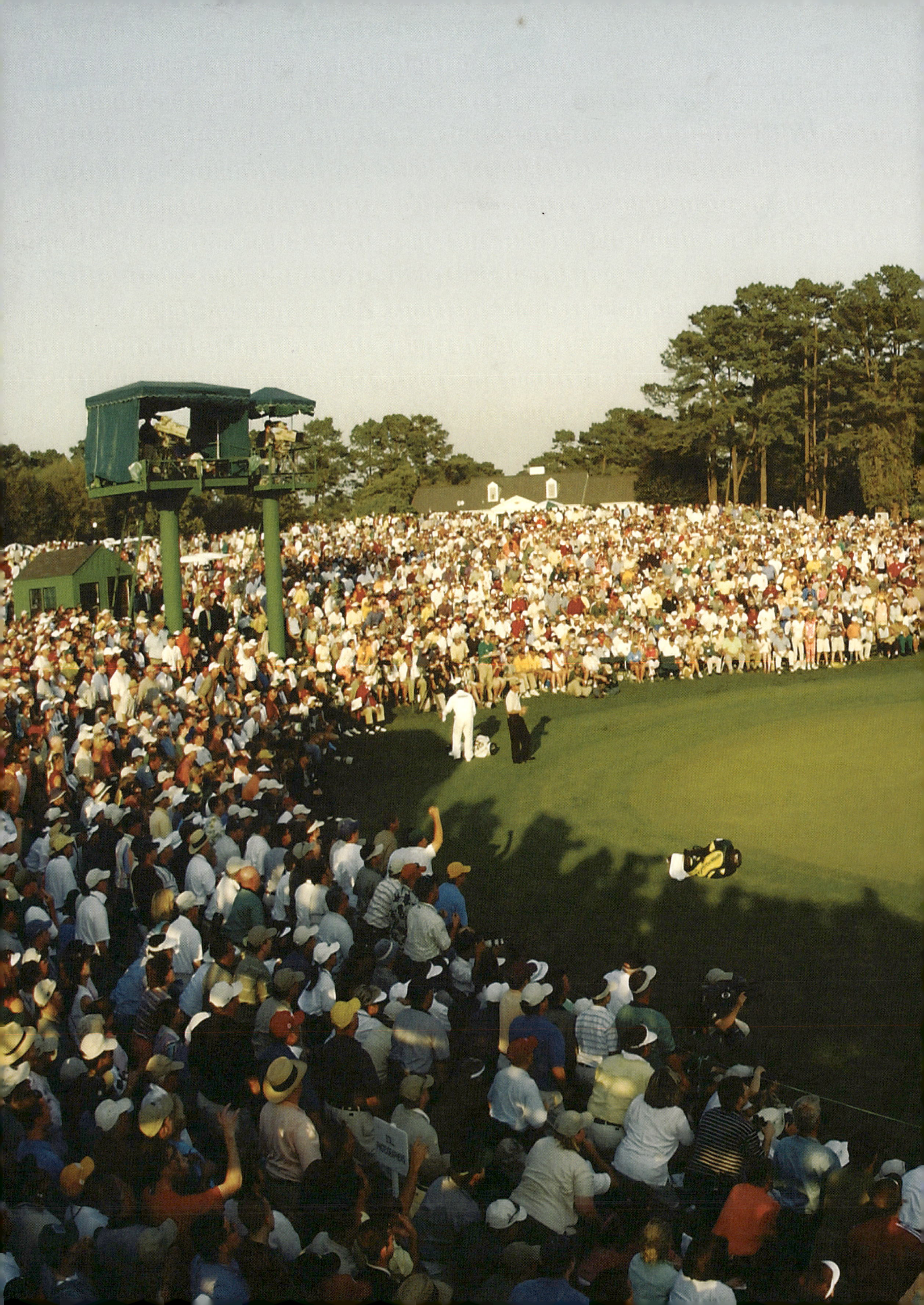